Parliamentary Elections in Israel
Three Case Studies

Parliamentary

Elections

in Israel

THREE CASE STUDIES

C. Paul Bradley

TOMPSON & RUTTER INC

Grantham, New Hampshire

First published 1985

by Tompson & Rutter Inc

Grantham, New Hampshire 03753-0297

Printed in the United States of America

*Library of Congress Cataloging
in Publication Data*

Bradley, C. Paul
   Parliamentary elections in Israel.

   Bibliography: p.
   Includes index.
   1. Israel. Keneset--Elections, 1977.
2. Israel. Keneset--Elections, 1981.
3. Israel. Keneset--Elections, 1984.
4. Israel--Politics and government--
1948-   . I. Title.
JQ1825.P365B715 1985   324.95694'054
ISBN 0-936988-11-8   85-1150

Contents

Preface

Political parties in Israel have deep roots in the prolonged prestate period (1897-1948). They competed for electoral preferment and political power both in the governing bodies of the World Zionist Organization (WZO), founded by Theodore Herzl, and the quasi-governmental institutions under the British mandatory regime, set up after World War I in Palestine. In 1948 a politically experienced elite assumed control of a fully sovereign state, based on a multiparty parliamentary system.

Israeli parties contest elections, form coalition governments, set government policies, exert extensive patronage powers, seek control of local governments, maintain close relations with trade unions, oftentimes engage in extensive publishing activities and in some cases run educational institutions. Since 1948 there has occurred some displacement of prestate party functions by state organs (see below). But party influence is still pervasive, and Israel is often defined as a "party-state."

Parliamentary elections, usually held every four years for control of the 120-member Knesset, provide useful data on this complex system. Until the electoral upheaval of 1977 the moderate so-

cialist Mapai/Labor party consistently won the
highest number of Knesset seats in eight parliamentary elections and won the right to form
every coalition government with a variable set of
partners. Its diminished plurality in the 1973
elections presaged its defeat in 1977. For the
first time in nearly three decades an alternative
government was formed by the rightwing Likud bloc,
led by the long-time opposition leader, Menachem
Begin. Some Israeli political scientists assert
that since 1973 Israel has been undergoing a realigning era, marked by a fundamental redistribu-
tion of political power. In this instance the
previously unbroken series of electoral victories
by the ascendant Labor party was decisively broken
in 1977. Whether a new dominant party will ultimately emerge is problematic. Three Knesset elections associated with this important transitional
phase will be examined in this study--those of
1977, 1981 and 1984.

Two sets of questions will be raised. The
first applies to each of the three elections.
What is the prevailing political climate which
sets the parameters for a given campaign? To what
extent can an incumbent government manipulate
external events to its advantage? Do foreign
policy and security issues prevail, or are they
subordinate to domestic policy? Do intra-party
factional divisions affect the electoral showing
of certain parties? To what extent do charismatic
leaders affect the outcome? Does a given election
significantly alter the balance of power between
the two leading parties? How do the lesser parties fare in the election outcome? How do the
religious parties maximize their gains in the
process of coalition formation? What is the pattern of concessions the governing party is compelled to make the lesser parties in narrow coalitions?

A second set of questions deal with longer term
trends. Is Israel moving towards a two-party
system, or will the realigning era take a less
definite form? Will a small cluster of third
parties continue to play a critical role in multi-

party coalitions or merely serve the interests of the larger parties? Do recent campaigns reflect an escalating level of violence, or will devices be found to contain these destructive forces harmful to Israeli democracy? What are the relative weights of the recent polarization trend and the counter-trend of fragmentation in the electorate? How strong are the visible centrifugal forces in the two major party blocs? How has the recent ethnic resurgence affected the divided religious camp? What trends can be detected in the ongoing leadership succession crises in both major parties? What is the relative weight of coalesence and fragmentation patterns among Israeli Arab voters?

An introductory chapter on the major features of the Israeli party system will precede separate chapters on each of the three parliamentary elections. For each election examined there will be a background section, an account of the campaign, an assessment of the results and a final section on the formation of a new post-election government. A short concluding chapter will summarize the most significant electoral trends in the 1977-1984 period.

LISTING OF ISRAELI
POLITICAL PARTY ABBREVIATIONS

CRM --- Citizen's Rights Movement

DFPE --- Democratic Front for Peace and Equality
         (Rakah)

DMC --- Democratic Movement for Change

ILP --- Independent Labor Party

NRP --- National Religious Party

PAY --- Poalei Agudat Yisrael

PLP --- Progressive List for Peace

I
An Introduction to the Party System

(1) Major Features

Israel's Movement-Type Parties

Historically Israel's parties have been more than electoral mechanisms and formulators of governmental policies.(1) They have assumed an exceptionally wide range of functions different from Western political parties. They have sponsored agricultural settlements--both strict collectives *(kibbutzim)* and less doctrinaire cooperatives *(moshavim)*; founded schools, hospital systems and operated medical insurance programs; set up their own industrial enterprises; issued daily newspapers and periodicals; organized youth movements, sports clubs and cultural centers. Before 1948 some parties had their own military and paramili-

---

1. Useful books on the Israeli political system include: *The Origins of the Israeli Polity*, D. Horowitz and M. Lissak (Chicago: University of Chicago Press, 1980); *Party and Politics in Israel: Three Visions of a Jewish State*, Rael Jean Isaac (New York: Longman, 1981); *The Government and Politics of Israel*, Don Peretz (Boulder, Colo.: Westview Press, 2nd edition, 1983); *Israel: The Embattled Ally*, Nadav Safran (Cambridge: Harvard University Press, 1978); and *Israel: Pluralism and Conflict*, Sammy Smooha (Berkeley: University of California Press, 1978).

tary organizations which were utilized against
their Arab opponents and in the last phase of the
struggle against the British mandatory power.
Large permanent staffs were required to manage
these diverse activities. Party-operated banks
were established to finance them, supplemented by
intensive fund-raising efforts which extended to
the overseas Diaspora.

The *Histadrut* or General Federation of Workers,
set up in 1920 under labor socialist auspices, is
an archtypical example of a multifunctional organization in the Israeli system. The Histadrut
is not only a very large trade union, but also has
provided housing projects, health services and
vacation resorts; set up a wide variety of cooperatives ranging from bus lines to construction
companies, schools and publishing houses; and
sponsored cultural activities, including theatri-
cal and musical groups. It was the initial sponsor of the clandestine *Haganah* which became the
principal defense force of prestate Jews. In the
1930s the socialist *Mapai* party (precursor to
Labor) gained control of the Histadrut apparatus,
which became its most important power base. There
was a significant overlap between key Mapai party
personnel and the labor organization. Over the
years Histadrut enjoyed a remarkable success, and
some of Mapai's rivals were impelled to set up
parallel organizations. By the early 1950s Histadrut employed nearly a quarter of the Israeli
labor force and accounted for 25 percent of its
gross national product. Two-thirds of Israel's
population was enrolled in its health service
(Kupat Holim).

Israel's service-oriented, movement-type parties represented an anomalous case of a fully
developed party system which preceded the creation
of a state bureaucracy. After independence these
"movement" parties retained the fixed loyalty of
their supporters to a surprising degree. This
partly explains the low "floating vote" which
characterized Israeli elections until the 1970s.
In seven elections before 1973 the relative voting
strength of the parties changed only slightly.

The Multi-Party System

Customarily two dozen or so parties put up
party lists in Knesset elections. Roughly half of
these win parliamentary seats, while only a half-
dozen parties exert significant influence in government. The marked fissiparous tendency of Israel's highly ideologized parties has since the
mid-1960s been partially offset by the formation
of electoral blocs, but with bloc member parties
often retaining a separate organizational identity. The two leading parties, the Labor alignment and the Likud bloc are important examples of
this trend.

In the prestate period political parties
coalesced in three distinct "camps"--the Labor-
socialist, the center-right and the religious.
The term "camp" implies the whole network of
institutions which Israel's movement parties
devised to integrate their supporters. Despite
internal party changes these three groupings
constitute the basic divisions in the present
party system.

(1)In a striking way the kibbutz--the agricultural collective--embodied the original ideology
of the *Labor-socialist camp*. The kibbutz represented an ideal societal form, which allowed many
Jews entering Palestine in successive waves of
immigration *(aliyot)* to resume their historical
way of life as an agricultural people. It en-
shrined certain values: the collective ownership
of land as opposed to private ownership; the
rejection of hired Arab labor, to which earlier
settler communities had resorted; the transcen-
dence of a money economy and a distributive system
based on need; communal raising of children; the
goal of egalitarianism and a just society; the
importance of manual work and attachment to the
soil; and concentration on small-scale cooperative
industry without distinctions between employer and
employee.

As early as the 1930s the Mapai party emerged
as the leading party in the Labor-socialist camp.

Initially it represented a merger of two divergent ideological strands--Marxism and the pioneering creed. It became the first governing party in independent Israel and remained so for 29 years. Confronted with the exigencies of nation-building, Mapai adopted an increasingly pragmatic approach and came to occupy a centrist position in the Israeli polity. For an extended period the Labor camp was subjected to an attritional process of fissure and formation of several splinter parties, derived from clashing ideologies. In the late 1960s Mapai took the initiative in forming a relatively unified Labor party, comprised of its former dissident *Rafi* faction on the right and its former partner, *Achdut Haavoda,* on the left. In 1969 the more doctrinaire Marxist *Mapam* party joined the Labor party factions to form the new "Alignment" *(Maarach).* Partly due to its mixed character the Labor party subsequently experienced serious internal strains (see below).

To the left of the Labor camp stood the pariah Communist party, which was never considered a potential member of any Israeli cabinet. In recent elections its chief political significance has been the sizable Arab vote which it has attracted.

(2)In the *center-right* camp there were by the mid-1960s two leading parties--Menachem Begin's militant-nationalist *Herut* (Freedom) party and the Liberal party, advocate of an untrammeled free enterprise system and individual rights. The bulk of Herut's electoral support came from the lower middle and working classes and increasingly from recent Jewish immigrants from Middle Eastern countries. The Liberal party, supported mostly by businessmen and professional groups, stood in the tradition of European bourgeois parties.

For 29 years after 1948 the Herut party was beyond the pale in Israeli politics--partly due to Prime Minister David Ben-Gurion's intercession (see below), partly because of its origins. Herut was heir to Vladimir Jabotinsky's deviant Zionist movement, known as the Revisionists, and the pre-

1948 underground organization, *Irgun Zvai Leumi* (National Military Organization), led by Begin. The charismatic Jabotinsky exerted an enormous influence on many young Jews in central and eastern Europe, including Begin's Poland. Jabotinsky created a great stir when he challenged the British redefinition of the Balfour Declaration in 1922 (accepted by the WZO), which excluded Transjordan from the original parameters of the promised Jewish National Home. In the Revisionist formulation *Eretz Israel* (Land of Israel) included territory both east and west of the Jordan River. After 1948 Herut incorporated this formula in its platform, and Begin became the leading advocate of full Israeli sovereignty over the entire original Mandate area.

Jabotinsky's insistence on the necessity of using force to create a Jewish state became the leit-motif of Begin's Irgun. The Irgun was identified with daring acts of terrorism, like the bombing of the King David Hotel in Jerusalem in 1946, where British officials were quartered. Ninety-one persons were killed, 45 injured.

Forced to disband the Irgun after independence, Begin organized the Herut as a political vehicle to articulate his nationalist creed. An early dramatic instance of Begin's special oppositional role was the imbroglio caused by the Government's decision to make a reparations agreement with West Germany in 1952. The Israeli government insisted the reparations would be used exclusively to help Israel absorb hundreds of thousands of survivors from the Hitlerite era. They were definitely not intended as "compensation" for millions of Holocaust victims. Many Israelis regarded the reparations as "blood money." In the bitter Knesset debate Begin attacked the reparations agreement as "the ultimate abomination, the like of which we have not known since we became a nation," and flailed Prime Minister Ben-Gurion as a "fascist and a hooligan."(2) Begin's supporters organized

2. *A History of Israel*, Howard M. Sachar (New York: A.A.Knopf, 1976), pp. 372-73.

a mass march on the Knesset, forced their way through a police cordon, setting fire to automobiles and throwing rocks at the Knesset building.

The next day Begin hinted at the prospect of civil war, when he claimed that he and his supporters were prepared "to give our lives" to forestall the reparations agreement. Ben-Gurion, asserting that the first steps had been taken "to destroy democracy in Israel," called out the Army to disperse the demonstrators and restore order.

Despite doctrinal differences between Herut and the Liberals--the latter were originally considerably less hawkish than the Herut, the two parties formed the *Gahal* bloc in 1965. The Liberals were seeking to overcome a factional split in their party, and Herut aspired to enhance its relatively weak Knesset position and facilitate its own legitimation. In 1965 the new bloc won only 26 seats. Prior to the 1973 election Gahal, at the instigation of General Sharon (see below), was enlarged to include several other rightist parties. The new Likud (Unity) bloc won eight more seats than had Gahal in the 1969 election; the Labor alignment lost six seats. Like its Labor counterpart Likud has been subject to serious factional disputes, especially after it assumed governmental power in 1977.

(3) In the *religious camp* the National Religious Party (NRP), comprised mostly of orthodox Jews, was for an extended period its leading party. In Knesset elections it consistently won between eight and ten percent of the vote and except for brief periods participated in every coalition government. It normally held the Cabinet posts of Religious Affairs and Interior. To a religious party control of the Religious Affairs ministry was especially important. It has built and maintained synagogues and *yeshivot* (rabbinical seminaries); appoints ecclesiastical personnel, including religious judges; issues directives for religious courts; and pays the salaries of nearly all Jewish religious functionaries, as well as those of other communities (including Muslim Arabs).

In the past decade the smaller party of ultra-orthodox Jews, *Agudat Yisrael*, has significantly increased its political influence. Originally anti-Zionist the Agudat has traditionally been wary of too close contact with a secular Zionist government. Since 1977 under Likud governments Agudat has aggressively pressed its parochial claims. Its governing body, the Council of Sages, does not permit its representatives in the Knesset (MK´s) to accept ministerial appointments, but it does hold important committee chairmanships in the Knesset. A third party, the labor branch of the Agudat, *Poalei Agudat Yisrael* (PAY), exerts only marginal influence.

The two major religious parties are strongly committed to the maintenance of the *religious status quo* agreement, arranged by Ben-Gurion, then head of the Jewish Agency, on the eve of independence.(3) It provided for continuation of certain practices and legislation passed during the Mandatory period, and was intended to reduce tensions between religious Jews and the secular majority. Its provisions were as follows: (1)the Sabbath would be the official day of rest in the Jewish state; (2)*Kashrut* (dietary) laws would be maintained in all public institutions; (3)religious school systems would be funded and maintained by the state; (4)public transportation would not operate in the country as a whole on Sabbaths and holidays; and (5)matters of personal status, primarily marriage and divorces would be governed by religious law. As a regular member of coalition governments the NRP has at times been willing to compromise on specific applications of the status quo agreement. Not having cabinet seats to lose, the Agudat maintains a maximalist position on its strict enforcement.

Both the NRP and Agudat have been mainly concerned with protecting the interests of their religious communities in the political sphere, especially the state funding of religious schools.

3. "Religion and Politics in Israel," Daniel J. Elazar and Janet Aviad, in *Religion and Politics in the Middle East* (Boulder, Colo.: Westview Press, 1981), p. 174.

Since the 1967 war the NRP has expanded its program to include forceful positions on territorial and foreign policy questions. The leadership of both parties has been dominated by Ashkenazi Jews.

In recent years there has been a substantial shift in Israeli public opinion away from secularism. Opinion studies show that although secularists once constituted the great majority of the population, they now account for not more than half, of whom only two-thirds are "strongly" secularist. The other half is comprised of one-third religionists who would regulate public life in accordance with religious law, and two-thirds of people who favor some links between religion and the state.(4) The primary cause for this shift was the post-1948 influx of religiously traditional Oriental Jews (see below).

At the outset of statehood Israel was confronted with several highly controversial issues of public policy which did not fit into narrow pro and con positions and helped perpetuate the pre-state multiparty system.

Israel's basic economic orientation--whether it should have a socialist, capitalist or a mixed economy, was widely debated. Leftist parties like Mapam favored an enlarged state sector, while rightist parties like the General Zionists (precursor to the Liberals) called for a greatly expanded private sector. Under the pragmatic Mapai party, post-1948 governments followed a middle course and adopted a flexible policy toward extensive private investment in Israel's mixed economy.

The question of a written constitution for the new state, which arose in 1949, proved highly contentious. Should Israel be organized as a secular state or a theocracy based on Jewish religious law? Religious Jews strongly opposed a written constitution which would perpetuate the prevailing values of secular Zionism. If the constitution were to explicate secular norms and values, participation in the government by the

4. Safran, op. cit., p. 209.

religious parties would be hampered. To avoid an open rupture between secularists and religionists, the device of a transitional set of "basic laws" which the Knesset enacted on a piecemeal basis was adopted.

The highly emotional issue of "who is a Jew" which raises the question of national identity erupted intermittently. In 1958 it took the form of a bitter dispute over whether in national registration procedures the citation of Jewish nationality could be separated from a registrant's religion. In ruling on a case of registering a child of a mixed marriage, the Minister of Interior (Bar-Yehuda) stated that a simple declaration by both parents that they considered the child Jewish sufficed, without reference to *halachic* (Jewish religious) law. Outraged religionists insisted on strict application of halachic law, which declared that an authentic Jew must be born of a Jewish mother or a convert to Judaism in accordance with orthodox ritual. They called for supportive demonstrations by orthodox Jews throughout the world. The two NRP ministers in the government angrily resigned. Prime Minister Ben-Gurion, anxious to avoid the collapse of his multiparty coalition, took recourse in polling of 43 scholarly experts on religious law, who affirmed the relevance of halachic law. The Interior ministry's original directive was revoked, future registrants had to meet the standard of orthodox Judaism and the NRP rejoined the government.

In the early 1950s the issue of Israel's appropriate foreign policy was widely debated. On the left the Communists and Mapam espoused a pro-Soviet position. The Herut and the General Zionists were adamantly opposed to further expansion of the Communist bloc and favored a close connection between Israel and the Western camp. The Mapai, whose representatives controlled the Foreign Ministry, initially advocated a policy of "nonidentification" with either of the two blocs. Once the Soviet Union adopted an unequivocally pro-Arab position in the mid-1950s, a national consensus favoring the West began to form. But

Israel's relations with the United States proved
intermittently stormy, as was the case when the
U.S. insisted on Israel's withdrawal from the
Sinai after its invasion of Egypt in 1956.

Two factors which partially mitigated the disruptive potential of these public controversies
were (1) the well-established prestate tradition
of bargaining and compromise associated with multiparty coalitions, and (2) Israel's almost continuous state of siege due to the implacable
hostility of its Arab neighbors.

A Proportional Electoral System

Israel's choice of an electoral system, based
on proportional representation rather than a
winner-take-all system, rested on solid precedents
from the prestate period. The World Zionist Organization (WZO), set up in 1897, was not attached
to any territorial entity, and its widely dispersed membership held sharply divergent views on
policy matters. Its Eastern European adherents,
for example, espoused a number of radical creeds
which flourished in prerevolutionary Russia. Initially the WZO represented only a small minority
of world Jewry, and could ill afford to antagonize
segments of its heterogeneous membership. A proportional representation system (PR) had the advantage of assuring a voice in WZO forums for even
small groups and attracting an expanding membership. The system was later extended to the Jewish
community *(Yishuv)* in Palestine which also had
marked ideological diversity. By 1948 most of the
established parties had acquired a vested interest
in the PR system so that its retention was a
foregone conclusion.(5)

In Knesset elections each contending party
presents a list of candidates, and an individual
voter selects a party list rather than specific
candidates. A special feature of the Israeli

---

5. *The Knesset: Parliament in the Israeli Political System,*
Gregory S. Mahler (London: Associated University Presses, 1981),
pp. 43-47.

system is that the whole nation constitutes a single electoral constituency. Throughout Israel the same party lists are presented to the electorate. The larger parties submit full lists with 120 names, although less than half actually win Knesset seats. Smaller parties that win few seats often submit shorter lists.

A relatively small number of party leaders compile the lists after prolonged bargaining among different party factions. Positions on a given list are rated as follows: (1)"safe" positions, roughly corresponding to the number of seats which the party won in the last Knesset election, minus about 10 percent; (2)"marginal" positions, corresponding to the seats won in the last election plus or minus about 10 percent; and (3)"symbolic" or "unrealistic" positions, whose holders are unlikely to win seats.(6) Party leaders are assigned positions at the top of the list which guarantee them Knesset seats. They frequently engage in intense competition for highest ranked order in the first half-dozen positions. While the electorate's choice is strongly party-oriented the parties will award top postions to especially popular leaders in order to attract the "floating" vote.

Rivalry is especially keen for positions that lie between the "safe" and "marginal" positions. If a given party expects to win 39 or so seats, the positions roughly between Nos. 37 and 42 on the list are highly valued, since electoral outcomes cannot be precisely predicted. The "unrealistic" positions are often assigned to promising younger party members, who expect to win "safer" positions in subsequent elections, as they prove their worth to the party.

The total number of valid votes cast in the election is divided by the number of Knesset seats (120). If, for example, a party wins 25 percent of the vote, it will be allotted 30 seats in the Knesset, and these go to the first thirty names on the party list. Any party winning a minimal one

6. Ibid., p. 45.

percent of the total vote is assured representation. Under a single national constituency very small parties win sufficient votes in scattered parts of the country to qualify under the one percent "threshold." In a winner-take-all system such parties would be deprived of parliamentary representation. Finally if a Knesset member (MK) dies or resigns, that seat will be assigned to the next lower name on the party list.

Israel's complicated electoral system has been subjected to repeated criticisms amidst calls for electoral reform. The PR system serves, it is argued, to perpetuate the highly fragmented multi-party system and delay the advent of a "more rational" two-party system. Third parties that hold the balance of power in a close election are seen to have a disproportionately influential voice in forming coalition governments. A handful of party leaders are said to exercise virtually dictatorial powers in compilation of party lists. Having a single national constituency underrepresents increasingly important regional interests, such as those articulated by the new development towns. Proponents of single member districts for each of the 120 seats under a British-type "first-past-the-post" system contend that such a reform would encourage a more majoritarian electorate. Some critics urge that the present one percent "threshold" be raised to five percent in order to discourage the formation of miniscule or "crank" parties. But periodic proposals of electoral reform provoke defensive reaction by entrenched smaller parties, which prevent radical electoral change.

Centralized Parties

From the prestate period to the present, Israeli parties have been highly centralized organizations. Some observers regard the Israeli system as even more centralized than the British. The concentration of power in the hands of relatively small numbers of national party leaders is evident

in their preeminent role in the nomination process, the conduct of electoral campaigns and in
enforcing party discipline in the Knesset.

The discretionary power which party leaders
exercise as members of small nomination committees
has been formidable. For an ambitious party member seeking a parliament seat, winning one of the
"safe" positions on a party list is crucial.
Without a Knesset seat participation in coalition
governments is virtually impossible. In the Knesset all members of a party bloc are bound to
support party-sponsored measures. MK´s who regularly ignore their party´s instructions risk being
assigned a lower position on the party list in the
next election or being "scratched" altogether.

When electoral blocs like the Labor alignment
and Gahal were formed in the 1960s, it was customary for a conference of the participating party
leaders to determine each party´s share of positions on the combined party lists. In the case of
the Labor alignment, for example, the top eight
positions were typically distributed as follows:
Nos. 1, 2 and 3 to Mapai as the leading party
faction; No. 4 to the smaller Rafi; No. 5 to the
Achdut Haavoda; Nos. 6 and 7 to Mapai; and No. 8
to Mapam. In this case the ration was 5-3 in
favor of Mapai. Since no set formula was devised,
bickering among Alignment leaders occurred frequently. The Likud bloc nearly fell apart in
1973, when two of its smaller parties disputed the
thirty-sixth and thirty-seventh positions on the
Likud list.

In the smaller parties that win only a few
Knesset seats, the leaders may resort to a prear-
ranged rotation in office. Halfway through the
Knesset term one of their MKs may resign and be
replaced by a representative of another party
faction.

In the 1970s dissatisfaction with elite-deter-
mined distributions became acute. Several parties
adopted less restrictive arrangements in the 1977
election (see below). But the nomination system
has been only marginally democratized.

Management of Knesset campaigns is controlled

by a relatively few party leaders. Electoral strategies are invariably formulated at the party headquarters in Tel Aviv. Increasingly campaigns are personalized by leaders of the Likud and Labor lists. This was strikingly evident in the 1981 campaign with the sharp contrast between the Likud's flamboyant Menachem Begin and his Labor challenger, the stolid Shimon Peres.

In the Knesset nearly all MKs in the governing coalition faithfully support the decisions of their parliamentary leaders, as do the MKs in the opposition parties. They are well aware of their dependency on the party center for a favorable position on future party lists, the requisite campaign funds and for assignment to important Knesset committees. Except for infrequent "free" votes determined by party leaders, most Knesset voting is party-based. Crossing the party line and joining another party group occurs infrequently.

The case of the one-time Labor MK, Shulamit Aloni, presents a slightly deviant example. She failed to follow formal party rules, tried to introduce legislation which her party had disapproved and spoke out openly against party policy. In the 1973 election she was left off the Alignment list. In this case the resourceful Aloni organized a new party--the Citizens Rights Movement(CRM)--which surprisingly won three Knesset seats.

Coalition Governments

No Israeli party has ever won majority control of the Knesset. This creates what some political scientists call a "minority situation, majority government," one in which a party with less than a majority of parliamentary seats joins with other minority parties to form a majority government.(7) The formation of multiparty coalitions necessarily involves compromises by the participants, which in turn dilutes the electorate's recently delivered

7. Ibid., p. 70.

mandate. With highly ideological parties which
are eager to retain their "core" support, compromises over future government policy are not made
easily. Prolonged negotiations typically lasting
between five and eight weeks are required before a
cabinet can be named, and thereafter dissatisfied
coalition partners may defect. In its first 25
years Israel had 18 governments.

Coalition theory in Israel stresses the concept
of a "dominant party"--i.e. the party with sufficient parliamentary resources to make its exclusion from governing coalitions impossible.(8)
Until 1977 that position was held by Mapai/Labor.
In the first six parliaments Mapai held at least a
third of the Knesset seats with no near rivals.
Its successor, the Alignment, controlled more than
40 percent of Knesset seats. Until 1973 Labor's
strongest opposition, the Gahal combination of
Herut and the Liberals, could muster only 26 votes
in the Knesset and was unable to mount an effective challenge against Labor. From its centrist
position Mapai/Labor enjoyed the further advantage
that parties on the extreme left (the Communists)
and on the extreme right (Herut) were too ideologically opposed to form a unified opposition.

In multiparty coalitions the dominant party is
required to make two kinds of "pay-offs" to its
prospective coalition partners: (1)policy concessions and (2)assignment of ministerial posts. In
the bargaining process these two tend to become
indistinguishable. A religious party like the NRP
may win both a commitment to pass a pork import
law and control over a ministry. A demand for an
economic ministry by Achdut Haavoda could be
"traded" for a less important post and a pledge by
the Government not to sell arms to West Germany.
Government departments have sometimes been shifted
and new ministries created, in order to attract
the requisite number of coalition partners.

The NRP, never holding more than 10-12 Knesset

8. "Coalition Myth and Reality," David Nachmias in *Elections in
Israel--1973*, Asher Arian, ed. (Jerusalem: Jerusalem Academic
Press, 1975), p. 243.

seats, has been an especially adept player in the coalition system, forming an "historic alliance" with the Labor party to maximize its gains. Despite its secular orientation Labor found it expedient to make policy concessions to the NRP on a relatively narrow range of religious subjects, in order to have a free hand in what it regarded as more important foreign and domestic policies. At the same time the NRP made the Religious Affairs and Interior ministries virtual NRP preserves.

A striking feature of the era of Labor-dominated coalitions was Labor's firm hold on five key ministries for nearly three decades. These included the office of Prime Minister, Defense, Finance, Foreign Affairs and Education, which together regulated more than 90 percent of the national budget. Control of these ministeries by a single party contributed an important element of stability in a system plagued by intermittent crises.

In the crisis period preceding the 1967 war a "wall-to-wall" national unity Government was formed, which represented a total of 111 MKs, including Begin's Herut party. Surprisingly this unwieldy coalition lasted until 1970, when Begin rejected a U.S.-sponsored cease-fire with Egypt. Two years later in the 1973 election the Herut-led Likud increased its Knesset representation from 31 to 39 seats. For the first time a party other than the Labor alignment became a feasible alternative government.

(2) Post-1948 Changes

For three and a half decades Israel had a tumultuous national history of nearly unrelieved crisis--five wars in the ceaseless conflict with the Arab states; the absorption of a million and a half new immigrants mostly from Asian and African states within a relatively short period; riots and demonstrations by Oriental Jews who perceive themselves as second-class citizens; the knotty prob-

26

lems inherent in ruling a sullen Arab population
in the West Bank and Gaza since 1967; recurrent
acts of terrorism by foreign-based groups linked
with the Palestine Liberation Organization(PLO);
the rise of a fervent religiosity among many Jewish settlers bent on achieving an enlarged *Eretz
Israel* (Land of Israel) in the occupied territories; and the search for a new generation of
national leaders to replace Israel's retiring
founding fathers.

   In such a rapidly changing society no party
system is immune from its own patterns of change.
In this section several important changes will be
summarized: the decline of movement-type parties
under the policy of statism; the new accent on
pragmatic politics; the growing importance of the
ethnic factor; Labor's "changing of the guard" in
the 1970s; the new "dove-hawk" political axis; and
the rise of highly influential extra-parliamentary
groups.

The Policy of Statism

   With the advent of independence the focus of
primary loyalty for many Israelis began to shift
from particularistic groups to the newly sovereign
state. The state was increasingly regarded as
representative of the whole citizenry and embodi-
ment of national unity. Previously an individual's basic commitments had typically been to his
kibbutz, Histadrut branch or to one of the political parties. Now the primacy of the state with
its expanding bureaucracy began to assert itself.
Some functions previously performed by political
parties and their affiliates were transferred to
state bodies. Even in the prestate period David
Ben-Gurion, the Labor-Zionist, embraced the strategy "from class to nation." As Israel's first
prime minister and dominant political leader for
nearly 20 years, Ben-Gurion was architect of the
policy of statism *(Mamlachtuit)*. In its implementation Ben-Gurion encountered strong resistance.

Creation of the IDF. First priority was given to the unification of the prestate defense forces under state control.(9) Four military units were involved: (1)Haganah, the largest of the militias, which had close ties to Mapai; (2)Palmach, Haganah's elite striking force, identified with the leftist Achdut Haavoda and Mapam parties; (3)the dissident offshoot of Haganah, Begin's Irgun Zvai Leuni; and (4)the "Fighters for Freedom of Israel"*(Lechi)*, widely known as the "Stern Gang," which split off from the Irgun. The Irgun and the Stern gang were committed to the aggressive use of force, including acts of terrorism, against Arab guerrillas and the British. At one point the Haganah was so incensed by the reckless strategy of the Irgun and Lechi that it tracked down and imprisoned hundreds of their members, turning over many of them to the British for deportation to Africa.

Ben-Gurion's showdown with the Irgun occurred in June 1948, only a month after independence. A shipment of arms intended for the Irgun arrived from Europe on the ship *Altalena*, just as the Government had accepted a United Nations truce which temporarily outlawed arms imports. The defiant Irgun persisted in unloading the arms. Ben-Gurion ordered the Army's intercession. The *Altalena* was sunk with loss of some Irgun lives, and the arms destroyed. Civil war in the midst of Israel's war with the Arabs was narrowly averted, when Begin reluctantly agreed to dissolve his underground organization. The *Altalena* incident had long-term political consequences. Ben-Gurion broke off relations with Begin and later refused to consider Begin's Herut party as a coalition partner.

Ben-Gurion's next step was to seek the dissolution of the Palmach, which precipitated a power struggle between Ben-Gurion's own Mapai party and the leftist Mapam. Ben-Gurion's statist policy clashed with Mapam's "movement" approach. Ben-Gurion's goal was the creation of a fully professional army under state control. Mapam regarded

9. Horowitz and Lissak, op. cit., p. 190.

the Palmach as an essentially political force, to
be mobilized in case of a future rightist coup and
preserve the Labor movement. A majority of the
Histadrut's executive committee accepted Ben-
Gurion's contention that jurisdiction in security
matters belonged exclusively to the Government.
Mamlachtuit was not always what it seemed on the
surface. Despite Ben-Gurion's protestations in
favor of a politically neutral army, a significant
number of the IDF's high-ranking officers had
Mapai connections and were political clients of
Ben-Gurion.(10) In this instance Mapai's party
interests coincided with a particular governmental
policy.

   A national education system. Bringing the
fragmented educational system under state control
aroused strong opposition, especially from religious parties. In the prestate period the British
allowed the Jewish Yishuv to set up its own educational system. Four main educational "streams"
were recognized, which represented ideologically
divided parties. They included the labor movement's system in which Mapai played a key role;
the "general" system supported by secular centrist
parties; and two religious systems. Each system
attempted to indoctrinate its students in its
preferred "way of life." Ben-Gurion argued that
the retention of this mixed system would lead to
"disintegration and endless splitting."(11)

   His proposal for a uniform education system
proved highly controversial, and passage of a
State Education Law was delayed until 1953. In
framing its legislative phraseology the Mapai
party accomplished a remarkable transfer of some
of the labor movement's traditional values to the
state as a whole. The new system of state education was intended to promote "trust in agricultural labor, craftsmanship and pioneer training" and

10. Yoram Peri stresses this point in *Between Ballots and Bullets:
Israeli Military in Politics* (Cambridge: Cambridge University
Press, 1983), pp. 61-64, 68-69.

11. *Mapai in Israel*, Peter Y. Medding (Cambridge: Cambridge University Press, 1972), p. 228.

build a society based on "freedom, equality, tolerance and mutual assistance."(12)

Despite the law's finely honed rhetoric only partial nationalization of education was achieved. The "general" and "labor" school systems were unified, but special provision was made for the two religious systems. Schools previously operated by the *Mizrachi* (precursor to the NRP) became "religious state schools" under Government supervision and subsidies, but with a religiously-oriented curriculum. A separate "independent" framework was set up for the ultra-orthodox Agudat schools, which also received state subsidies. All teachers in the two religious systems were required to be religious Jews.

Depoliticizing labor exchanges. Labor exchanges, established by the Histadrut in the pre-state period, were originally politicized. In accordance with Histadrut practice they were manned by political appointees. Mapai, the dominant party in the Histadrut, gained the majority of positions in all exchanges, and Mapai party members were favored in many placements. Other Histadrut parties played a modest role in operation of the exchanges. In an important policy innovation in the mid-1950s, it was decided to place the exchanges under full state control. The official rationale was that state-operated exchanges facilitated overall economic planning, but the new policy was partly a response to the increasingly widely held view that job placement in Israel should be divorced from party affiliation.(13)

Towards a merit system. The depoliticizing of appointments to Government positions was only gradually applied. Immediately after independence most recruitment to new government departments was party-based. Each coalition partner regarded the ministries it was assigned as legitimate party spoils with loyal party members favored for most

12. Ibid., p. 229.

13. Ibid., p. 232.

jobs. The Ministry of Religion, for example,
became an NRP bailiwick. Mapai, controlling the
most important departments, was the primary beneficiary of this system. Gradually the Government's role in building a modern industrial
economy required a more "rational" system. Technical experts came to be more valued than party
hacks. New civil service regulations, based on
merit, applied, however, only to newly created
jobs, so most party appointees remained in their
established positions. Obviously a longer period
was necessary for full implementation of a merit
system.

In summation effective implementation of
statist policies was heavily dependent on Ben-
Gurion's bold conceptualization of national
requirements; the imperatives of an almost continuous national emergency; the government's increasing use of economic planning; and the expanding
role of technology in an industrial society.
Party influences were not, however, easily
removed.

Immigrant Absorption and Pragmatic Politics

The national project of processing thousands of
new immigrants after 1948 provided fresh opportunities for recruitment and mobilization by the
leading political parties.(14) Nearly 700,000
immigrants entered Israel between 1948 and 1952,
more than doubling its Jewish population, and a
similarly large number followed in the next fif-
teen years. There were two main sources of immigration: the remnant of European Jewry,
survivors of the Holocaust; and second, Jews from
Islamic countries in the Middle East and North
Africa such as Iran, Iraq, Yemen, Morocco and
Tunisia. These Oriental/Sephardic Jews had a
radically different cultural background from the
Ashkenazi population of European and American
extraction which had dominated the prestate

14. Horowitz and Lissak, op. cit., pp. 200-206.

aliyot.(15)   Many Oriental Jews were poorly educated and lacked vocational training, which Israel's modernizing economy required.   Their
arrival in huge numbers presented Israel with an
acute problem of social integration, which even
today has not been resolved.

Initially the absorption machinery was controlled by the Jewish Agency and manned by party
representatives.   They were selected on a "party-
key" basis in rough approximation of the parties'
prestate strength, which gave Mapai representatives a substantial advantage.   At the outset
immigrants from Europe and North Africa spent a
prolonged period in transit camps in Italy and
France before entering Israel.   Party emissaries
were sent abroad to organize these immigrant
groups.   There was the special case of Yemen's
47,000 Jews, nearly all of whom were flown directly to Israel during 1949 and 1950 under "Operation
Magic Carpet."   In immigrant camps in Israel the
new arrivals were dependent on party personnel for
virtually all their needs.   Health services were
provided by the Kupat Holim (Sick Fund) of the
Histadrut, in which Mapai held an absolute majority.   Religious services were provided by the Jewish Rabbinate and Ministry of Religious Affairs,
which had close ties to the religious parties.
Immigrants assigned to party-oriented agricultural
settlements were targets for party recruitment.
In the two score or so "development towns" set up
for immigrants, party representatives served as
intermediaries for securing jobs, business licen-
ses and housing credit.

In the prestate period the parties had relied
heavily on sophisticated ideological appeals to
attract support from a small, relatively homoge-
neous population of mostly European Jews.   In the
greatly enlarged and more heterogeneous electorate

15. The terms "Oriental" and "Sephardic" are used interchangeably
in Israeli political parlance.   More strictly Sephardic Jews are
those influenced by Spanish culture, who settled both in Western
and Muslim countries.   In this study Israeli Jews emigrating from
Muslim states after 1948 are referred to as "Oriental" Jews.   Ashkenazi Jews came to Israel mainly from Eastern and Central Europe
and in fewer numbers from North America.

after 1948, the parties adopted a more pragmatic
approach. There was a perceptible decline in
their emphasis on abstract ideology. More and
more the parties became political machines for
effectively organizing thousands of new voters,
most of whom were unfamiliar with the complex
workings of a multi-party democracy. Oriental
Jews, most of whom came from authoritarian regimes
in Arab states, were especially susceptible to
"guidance" by the established parties.

Despite the influx of several hundred thousand
new voters the distribution of electoral support
for the leading parties remained remarkably stable
between 1949 and 1955. Electoral shifts which did
occur originated mainly in the votes of long-time
Israeli residents rather than among the new immigrants. The use of the proportional "party key"
in immigration absorption reinforced the electoral
divisions of the prestate period and discouraged
the rise of ethnically-based parties.

Gradually the immigrants' dependence on party
machines was lessened. Most immigrant camps were
closed by the late 1950s. Most immigrants were
eventually absorbed in the large cities--Tel Aviv,
Haifa and Jerusalem, partly because of the high
population turnover in the agricultural settlements and development towns.(16) In big urban
centers there were fewer direct contacts with
party representatives. The relative openness of
urban life gradually modified the immigrants'
voter preferences. In the 1960s there was some
decline in the previously large number of immigrants voting for the Mapai party. The Herut
party was the chief beneficiary of this shift,
which became more marked in the 1973 and 1977
elections.

16. Horowitz and Lissak, op. cit., pp. 204 and 207.

1. The Jewish Sector

By 1967 the Oriental/Sephardic Jews constituted
55 percent of Israel's Jewish population. Every
social index indicated that their position was
disadvantageous in relation to the Ashkenazi.(17)
Collectively they are often referred to as the
"second" Israel. Oriental Jews hold a disproportionately small number of higher status, better
paying professional, technical and administrative
jobs and are overrepresented in lower status blue-
collar jobs. The average income for Orientals is
about half that of the Europeans. Most Orientals
live in ethnically segregated areas in the big
urban centers, and many occupy substandard housing. Twice as many Ashkenazi youth graduate from
high school as Orientals, many of whom leave
school early and join the labor force. Fewer than
ten percent of university graduates are Orientals.
Ashkenazi Jews constitute Israel's political
elite. In the first 25 years only three out of a
total of 64 cabinet members were Orientals. They
are regularly underrepresented in the Knesset. In
the IDF few Orientals hold officer positions beyond the rank of captain.
During the massive influx of new immigrants in
the 1950s, Oriental Jews were generally politically passive. A new activist phase was triggered by
an incident in Wadi Salib, a crowded slum area in
Haifa heavily populated by Moroccan Jews, in July
1959. Violence erupted when a barroom brawl resulted in a police shooting. A Mapai electoral
rally was also disrupted by demonstrators. An
investigatory Government commission reported that
many urban Moroccan Jews bitterly resented dis-
criminatory practices in housing and jobs, which
they claimed were widespread. A small, militant
organization of North African Immigrants was
formed to articulate, without notable success, a
wide range of ethnic grievances. A decade later

17. Peretz, op. cit., pp. 54-63.

more serious ethnic disturbances marked the formation of the Black Panthers organization, which
will be considered in the section on extra-parliamentary groups below.

Political parties based on ethnic groups have
been generally ineffectual. There are several
contributory factors. They have been inadequately
financed and inexpertly organized. Often they
have been weakened by factional divisions, as when
the Blue-White Panthers split off from their parent organization. Post-1948 immigrants were aggressively recruited by established parties that
had competitive advantages over transient ethnic
organizations. The two largest parties produced
outstanding charismatic leaders, Mapai's Ben-
Gurion and Herut's Begin, who commanded national
attention and whose support cut across ethnic
lines. Coalition parties have substantial benefits and patronage to exchange for votes. Established parties made effective use of cooption of
dissident ethnic leaders. Once ethnic militance
was expressed, the older parties assigned a number
of places in the lower range of "safe seats" on
their electoral lists to Oriental Jews. The major
role which Oriental voters played in the Likud's
victory in 1977 indicates that the near-term prospects of narrowly based ethnic parties are bleak.

2. The Arab Sector

The position of the half million Arabs in a
Zionist Jewish state is highly anomalous.(18)
During the War of Independence about 700,000 Arabs
fled the country, leaving only about 150,000 in
Israel. The rhetoric of Israel's Declaration of
Independence guaranteeing all citizens including
the Arabs "full social and political equality" was
undermined by the war. The concentration of the
Arab population in strategically located areas
like the Galilee, the "Little Triangle" bordering

18. Two informative books on Israel Arabs are Jacob M. Landau's
The Arabs in Israel (London: Oxford University Press, 1969) and
Ian Lustick's *Arabs in the Jewish State* (Austin: University of
Texas Press, 1980).

Jordan and Negev raised serious security questions for the Government. Between 1948 and 1966 a repressive military administration was imposed on the Arabs. They were required to have passes, issued by the army, to travel within certain points. They were subject to army search and seizure, arbitrary arrest, banishment to other villages and expulsion from Israel. An Absentee Property Law authorized land seizures from persons who had been in "enemy" territory during specified periods, which was indiscriminately applied to Israeli Arabs. By the 1960s the Arabs had lost about two-thirds of their agricultural land, and bitter disputes over compensation were frequent. A significantly large number of Arabs were forced to leave farming and take low-status jobs as in the construction industry in the Jewish urban sector.

Israel's occupation of the West Bank and Gaza had a major impact on Israeli Arabs. Prior to 1967 they had been physically isolated from major developments in the Arab world and had virtually no contact with the million Palestinians under Jordanian administration. After 1967 they reestablished close relations with relatives and friends in the occupied territories. At close hand they observed the expanded operations of Palestinian guerrilla organizations and countermeasures taken by the Israelis--deportations, mass arrests and housing demolitions. Some Israeli Arabs gave shelter and support to Palestinian guerrillas, which provoked frequent searches by Israeli police. As more Israeli Arabs were exposed to Palestinian nationalist ideology, they increasingly identified themselves as Palestinian and questioned Israel's legitimacy as a national state. The cumulative effect was to "Palestinianize" many Israeli Arabs and undermine their ultimate integration in Israeli society.

Two aspects of the political behavior of Israeli Arabs require mention: their participation in "affiliated lists" drawn up by Zionist Jewish parties; and their increased support after the mid-1960s of the anti-Zionist *Rakah*, the Israeli Communist Party.

After 1948 the Arabs comprised one of the largest blocs of uncommitted voters.(19) Surprisingly their turnout in Knesset elections averaged over 80 percent. With the relatively small "floating vote" that typified early Knesset elections, the Arab vote assumed special importance for Jewish parties. Some adopted the practice of "affiliated lists" of Arab candidates, which were intended to elicit Arab votes. These lists were comprised mostly of local notables in Arab villages, especially the heads of influential clans (hamulas), who could deliver sizable blocs of local voters. In return they received certain benefits and in the case of those on the lists of coalition parties, some governmental patronage. Some clan leaders were reputed to receive checks for amounts calculated on a per-vote-promised basis, which could be cashed only after election day.(20)

The Mapai's use of affiliated lists proved quite successful. As the governing party it had substantial benefits to distribute. Its control of the Histadrut (to which Arab workers were admitted after 1959) also helped Mapai win Arab support. In some elections Mapai sponsored two or three affiliated Arab lists in order to exploit traditional hamula rivalries. In the nine Knesset elections between 1949-1977 a minimum of one and a maximum of five Arabs were elected on labor-affiliated lists. In the Knesset Arab MKs play an extremely modest role, only occasionally voicing Arab grievances. Until the 1977 election Labor received an average of 53 percent of the Arab vote. Even the NRP comprised of orthodox Jews received some Arab votes, due to the benefits it distributed, when the NRP controlled such ministries as Religious Affairs, Interior or Social Welfare.

In 1965 a split occurred in the Israeli Communist party. The Rakah faction shortly became the only influential Communist party. Despite its mixed Jewish-Arab leadership Rakah won increased

19. Lustick, op. cit., pp 112-13.

20. Ibid., p. 229.

electoral support from young, educated Arabs, who perceived Rakah as an indisputably anti-Zionist party and virtually the only one that devoted substantial attention to Arab concerns. Although mostly indifferent to Marxist ideology, many Arabs voted for Rakah as a protest against governmental policies they disliked.

In its Arab-language newspaper Rakah champions the Palestinian cause and publicizes unpopular policies of Israeli occupation officials: the wide use of administrative detention, deportation of PLO members and the steady expansion of Jewish settlements in the occupied territories. By organizing rallies and raising funds for families of jailed Palestinians, Rakah further activates Arab nationalism.

Between 1965 and 1973 the percentage of the Arab vote for Rakah increased from 23.6 to 37 percent. In 1977 the Arab vote for the Communist-led Democratic Front rose to 49.4 percent.

Leadership Succession Crises

Subject to intergenerational tensions and with no fixed terms for party officials, Israeli parties periodically undergo leadership crises. In the case of Mapai, leadership was long shared by members of the second *aliyah* (1905-12) and a younger group who arrived in the third *aliyah* (1919-23). Leaders of these two groups dominated the top leadership posts after independence. The older group was engaged in high-level decision-making, while the younger group controlled the Mapai party machine.(21) When the older group began to leave political life in the late 1950s Mapai faced a destabilizing succession crisis.

Initially it took the form of a factional struggle between the "Young Guard" and the veteran party leaders that controlled the party ma-

21. See Arian's article in *Israel at the Polls: The Knesset Election of 1977*, Howard R. Penniman, ed. (Washington, D.C.: The American Enterprise Institute, 1979), p. 294.

chine.(22) Both personality clashes and policy
disagreements fed the rivalry. The well-educated
Young Guard was impatient to move quickly into top
leadership positions. Their technocratic outlook
contrasted sharply with the traditional labor
socialist views that prevailed in the party machine. The Young Guard demanded more democratic
party procedures, reform of the PR electoral system and further extension of statist measures,
including the nationalization of Histadrut health
services.

Young Guard leaders had close relations with
Ben-Gurion, especially Moshe Dayan, the principal
war hero of the 1956 war, and Shimon Peres, a key
official in the Defense Ministry. The veterans
were displeased when Ben-Gurion attempted to bring
Dayan directly into the Cabinet, after he left the
army as Chief of Staff in 1957.

After Ben-Gurion's resignation in 1963, his
opponents in Mapai arranged the entry of the leftist Achdut Haavoda party to neutralize the Young
Guard. The expanded organization was approved at
a party conference in 1965 by a 60-40 margin.
Ben-Gurion then organized an opposition splinter
party known as *Rafi*. In the Knesset election
which followed, Rafi won only 7.9 percent of the
popular vote compared to the 36.7 percent of its
parent Mapai party.(23) Later Rafi leaders Dayan
and Peres rejoined Mapai. Ben-Gurion, still a
dissident, formed the State party, which proved
politically inconsequential.

A new phase in Labor's leadership crisis developed in the aftermath of the Yom Kippur War in
1973. Prime Minister Golda Meir and Defense Minister Moshe Dayan came under heavy fire for their
responsibility in Israel's poor showing in the
early stages of the war. The Labor party vote in
the election, held in December 1973, significantly
declined.

22, "The Decline of the Israeli Labor Party: Causes and Significance," Myron J. Aronoff (Penniman volume on the 1977 election),
p. 121.

23. Ibid, p. 122.

The critical report of the special commission (Agranat) on the conduct of the 1973 war provoked fresh attacks on Dayan and Meir. Mrs. Meir shortly resigned. A virtual newcomer to active party politics, Yitzchak Rabin, was named Meir's successor. Rabin had served as IDF chief of staff in the 1967 war and later as ambassador to the United States. In a hotly contested vote for party leader Rabin defeated Peres, representing the Rafi faction.

Rabin was the first Israeli Prime Minister that had not been closely associated with the Mapai party. As the first Israel-born *(sabra)* head of government, Rabin symbolized generational change in the national political leadership. In his short tenure of two years Rabin built a new party coalition, which tended to ignore the old party factions. Peres' assumption of Labor's leadership in 1976 indicated, however, that Labor's prolonged leadership crisis was not yet resolved.

Begin's Herut party was also subject to leadership crises. After the party's relatively poor showing in the 1965 election, Begin's leadership was challenged by Shmuel Tamir, an Irgun veteran. Tamir was defeated after a bitter fight and later suspended from Herut for a year. One of Begin's supporters said he would "rather die in the desert with Begin than sit in a government with Tamir."(24) Later Tamir left Herut and organized the small Free Center party. Ezer Weizman following his retirement from the Air Force joined Herut and made a bid for party leadership in 1969 which was also defeated.

The Territorial Question

The 1967 war and Israel's territorial acquisitions introduced a new divisive component in the national political dialogue--the territorial question. Party leaders were forced to deal with a host of controversial questions: What was to be

24. Issac, op. cit., p. 150.

the future of the several territories--the West
Bank (known in Israeli parlance as Judea and Samaria), the Gaza Strip, the Syrian Golan Heights,
the Egyptian Sinai? Was their acquisition just
the first step toward regional hegemony by Israel?
Which of these should be retained by Israel and
for what reasons--security, strategic location,
ideological, or some combination of these? If
withdrawal were decided upon, what were to be the
conditions? Should Israeli Jews be free to settle
there, and if so, in what areas and in what numbers? A new hawk-dove axis developed in the electorate. "Hawks" were defined as uncompromisingly
opposed to Israeli withdrawal and in favor of
virtually unlimited Jewish settlements. "Doves"
favored some kind of territorial compromise and
restricted Jewish settlements in the occupied
territories. These differences cut across party
lines, and in several instances created new intra-
party factions.

After 1967 Herut upheld Israel's claim to Judea, Samaria and the Gaza Strip, and insisted on
the right of Jews to settle anywhere in these
territories. The Herut position prevailed in the
Likud.

Although the NRP had initially favored some
kind of territorial compromise, the party was
increasingly influenced by its hawkish "Young
Guard" faction. Prior to the 1973 election the
NRP leadership stated that it could not participate in a government that accepted "relinquishment
of parts of Eretz Israel--the heritage of our
fathers."

The Labor alignment was seriously divided on
the territorial question, as the 1969 election
campaign revealed. Its leftist Mapam affiliate
initially favored a limited withdrawal policy,
restricted to the Jordanian West Bank. Many Labor
doves were concerned that permanent retention of a
heavily populated Arab region would ultimately
undermine Israel's Zionist character, especially
since the Arab birth rate was considerably higher
than that of Israeli Jews. Moshe Dayan, a hardliner, insisted Israel was in the West Bank by

"right and not on sufferance, to visit, live and
to settle."(25)   Israel should maintain military
bases there, he argued, and prevent the entry of
an Arab army.   Like other Alignment leaders
Dayan's position on the ultimate disposition of
the territories was ambiguous, to be determined in
the context of a final peace settlement.

Prior to the 1973 election the Labor party,
despite continued intra-party differences, appeared likely to endorse a hawkish position not
dissimilar from the Likud's.   At a party convention held before the Yom Kippur War, the so-called
"Galili Document," favored by party hawks, was
hotly debated.   It recommended an ambitious four-
year plan of economic development for the occupied
territories, whose political status would remain
unchanged.(26)   Substantial government funds were
to be allocated for improving the Arab infrastructure and expanded social services.   Most importantly the territories were to be opened up for
large-scale Jewish investment.   The use of tax
relief and government loans was intended to encourage Jewish entrepreneurs to set up industrial
plants there.   Private acquisition of Arab lands
and property would be accelerated and Jewish settlements expanded.   Party doves denounced the
Galili plan as "creeping annexation."

Immediately after the war with the Meir government on the defensive, the Labor party shelved the
Galili plan and adopted a more moderate policy.
It called on a peace settlement that would insure
"defensible borders," based on territorial compromise.   For the first time the party recognized the
need for a "Palestinian identity," presumably
under the aegis of a Jordanian-Palestinian state.
Future Jewish settlements would be limited to
those dictated by security considerations.   The
earlier references to large investments and land
acquisitions were dropped.   Following a bitter

25. "Israel's 1969 Election: The Visible and the Invisible," Don
Peretz, *Middle East Journal* 24, no. 1 (1970): 37.

26. "The War Election and Israel's Eighth Knesset, " Don Peretz,
Middle East Journal 28, no. 2 (1974): 113-14.

debate, Labor adopted the new program. In the
ensuing campaign Likud attacked the Alignment's
program as "leading to surrender and endangering
the nation's survival."

Extraparliamentary Groups

In the wake of the 1967 war there emerged a
number of extra-parliamentary groups on both the
left and the right, which were deeply dissatisfied
with the Israeli Establishment--the political
parties and associated institutions that had dominated the country since the 1930s. The sources of
their disaffection were varied: the blandness of
political life resulting from the decline of ideology; the concentration on materialist goals and
personal enrichment with a concomitant loss of
idealistic commitment; the mounting evidence of
corruption in public life; the exclusionist practices of the Ashkenazi elite; equivocations on the
territorial definition of the Israeli state.
These groups shared in common a rejection of traditional politics and resort to direct action
tactics: street demonstrations, confrontations
with the police and in a few cases acts of terrorism. Overall the rightist groups proved more
effective than those of the left.

Leftist groups. Three of these represented the
avant-garde of the dovish position on the territorial question: *Matzpen* (the Israeli Socialist
Organization), *Siah* (New Israeli Left) and *Yesh*,
an Arab-Jewish student group. These organizations
were activated to protest the Labor government's
long delay in initiating peace negotiations with
Arab countries. Their agitational efforts were
concentrated on the campuses of Israel's three
major universities--Jerusalem, Tel-Aviv and Haifa,
and included mass demonstrations, sit-ins, teach-
ins and circulation of protest petitions. In the
end their activities had virtually no influence on
governmental policy, and according to one observer
were only a pale imitation of student revolts in

the Western democracies in the late 1960s.(27)

The special case of the Black Panthers. In
contrast to leftist groups preoccupied with the
territorial question, the Black Panthers, organized in 1971 and borrowing their name from the
well-known extremist organization of American
blacks, was exclusively concerned with the depressed state of Oriental Jews living in urban
slum neighborhoods. Led by a small group of young
Orientals from the Morasha slum area of Jerusalem
the organization spread to other urban centers.
The Black Panthers´ objective was to mobilize
protests against their poor housing conditions,
poor education and mistreatment of juvenile de-
linquents of Oriental origin. They were especially incensed by the Government´s policy of offering
the best housing and job opportunities to very
recent immigrants, most of whom were Soviet and
Western Jews. These favored immigrants could buy
cars and appliances without paying regular sales
taxes, were exempted from income taxes during
their first years in Israel and were able to
secure cheap mortgages for their homes. The Black
Panthers relied heavily on mass demonstrations,
which frequently ended in violent clashes with
police.

In this instance the Labor government was compelled to attend to the grievances articulated by
the Black Panthers. A special investigation committee was set up, which rendered a critical report on urban living conditions. A special
Adviser to the Prime Minister was created, and a
permanent ministerial committee was set up to
administer an extensive remedial program. The
Black Panthers were subsequently weakened by factional disputes and formation of rival groups.

The protest against the conduct of the 1973 war.
This amorphous protest movement was initiated by
an obscure IDF officer, Captain Motti Ashkenazi, a
field commander in the Suez Canal campaign. Many
of his soldiers had died, as a result of what he
regarded as a serious blunder by military authori-

27. "Extreme Politics in Israel," Ehud Sprinzak, *The Jerusalem
Quarterly*, no. 5 (Fall 1977): 39.

ties. In February, 1974, he began a one-man sit-in in front of the Prime Minister's office. There he would sit, he announced, until Defense Minister Dayan resigned. Ashkenazi's vigil prompted the formation of a larger spontaneous protest movement, which sponsored demonstrations, anti-government sit-ins and teach-ins and public petitions. The largest demonstration held at the Prime Minister's office on March 24, 1974, attracted about 6,000 participants.

A noteworthy feature of this loosely organized movement, which was called "Our Israel," was the elitist character of its membership. It included reserve army officers of all ranks, senior managers in economic enterprises, scientists, intellectuals, white-collar professionals and members of well-established kibbutzim and moshavim.(28) They flocked to Jerusalem to participate in a series of demonstrations. Although the movement's main target was the Labor government, it was supported by leading members of the Labor party. "Our Israel" was widely considered to be a major factor in the reorganization of the Labor government in 1974 after the departure of Meir and Dayan. When the Cabinet changes were effected, the movement dissolved. But it laid the groundwork for the important Peace Now movement, which subsequently proved capable of mobilizing mass demonstrations on issues of peace and war.

The new settler movement. Israel's territorial expansion in 1967 stimulated a fresh surge of expansionist nationalism. The newly conquered territories became the target of a new settler movement led by devoutly religious Jews.

Its first organizational vehicle was the Movement for Greater Israel, organized shortly after the 1967 war. Its membership represented remarkably divergent sectors; disaffected members of the Israeli Establishment; a dissident Labor kibbutz federation; nationalist poets and literary figures; and some demobilized soldiers.(29) Their

28. Ibid., p.41.

29. *Radical Dissent in Contemporary Israel: Cracks in the Wall,* David J. Schnall (New York: Praeger Publishers, 1979), p. 140.

main concern was to insure Israel's retention not
only of the West Bank and Gaza, but also the Golan
and parts of the Sinai peninsula. In 1968 they
became identified with the new Jewish settlement
at Kiryat Arba near the Arab city of Hebron,
destined to be a flashpoint of future Jewish-Arab
clashes. After its electoral list in the 1969
Knesset election fared poorly, interest in the
settler movement declined for several years.

The Yom Kippur War in 1973 reactivated the
settler movement and led to the formation of *Gush
Emunim* (Bloc of the Faithful). Initially the
Gush functioned as an NRP faction with close ties
to its militant Young Guard. Early in 1974 following the Knesset election, it withdrew from the
NRP and functioned as an independent organization.
Spiritual leadership for the new movement was
provided by Rabbi A. Y. Kook and his son, Rabbi
Zvi Yehuda Kook, whose yeshiva for higher Judaic
studies in Jerusalem was attended by many Gush
leaders. The Kooks redefined Zionism in strongly
religious terms. In Herzlian Zionism the religious component was severely subordinated to the
secular element. The Kooks viewed the advent of
the Israeli state as the beginning of a divinely
inspired redemptive process(30) Jewish settlement
of "The Land" (i.e. the post-1967 Greater Israel)
was an important indicator of the unfolding of the
redemptive process. Withdrawal from the newly
conquered territories would, the Kooks argued,
directly contravene God's Will, and cause the
interruption or at worst the cessation of the
redemptive process. Each successful settlement on
the West Bank represented a step toward the final
culmination of a Third Jewish Commonwealth. The
Kooks urged religious Jews to work with secular
Zionists in settlement activities on grounds that
both would be acting as agents of a divine will.
In preaching his messianic creed, the elder Rabbi
Kook distanced himself from secular political
parties which provided the Gush with a precedent

30. "Gush Emunim: Politics, Religion and Ideology in Israel,"
Kevin A. Avruch, *Middle East Review* 11, no. 2 (1978-79): 27.

for their own disassociation from established parties.

Gush Emunim has proved the most effective of the extra-parliamentary groups. Its methods of direct action included mass demonstrations, holding marches in the West Bank (one in 1976 attracted 20,000 supporters), establishment of illegal settlements and recently involvement in a secret terrorist group (see Chapter IV). Its well-educated leadership maintains an exceptionally high elan and has demonstrated superior organizational ability. Although Gush was in its origins a spiritual movement, it has attracted substantial support from secular nationalists. These include veterans of the earlier (pre-1948) settler movement in Labor's kibbutzim and moshavim. For them Gush projects a vigorous revival of the virtually defunct Labor-socialist pioneer tradition. It should be recalled that many of the early settlements were set up in defiance of the British mandatory authority as were some of the Gush settlements under the Rabin government. The latter favored only settlements that could be justified on security grounds--i.e. near vital borders, rather than on ideological (spiritual) grounds. Indiscriminate Jewish settlements beyond the pre-1967 "Green Line" would, according to Rabin, jeopardize a final settlement of the Arab-Israeli conflict. In 1976 Gush attempted to hold Jewish services in Hebron's Tomb of the Patriarchs, sacred to Muslims. Widespread rioting broke out in the Arab West Bank, requiring police intervention.

With the advent of the first Begin government Gush Emunim enjoyed a very considerable increase in its political influence and achieved a certain legitimation. In May, 1977, the new Prime Minister made his first post-election speech at a Gush settlement, proclaiming Judea and Samaria (the West Bank) to be part of Israel. The new Government actively collaborated in setting up seven new Gush settlements. This trend toward *de facto* legitimation of the Gush was checked, however, when the Begin government ordered the dismantling of settlements in the Sinai under Israel's 1979 peace treaty with Egypt.

II
The 1977 Election

(1)   Disarray in the Labor Camp

The Collapse of the Rabin Government

In a period of five months prior to the 1977 election the Rabin government was subject to an astonishing number of setbacks which augured ill for Labor's electoral prospects.

A major crisis for the government developed from a routine public ceremony in December 1976, marking the arrival of Israel's first shipment of F-15s from the United States.   The round of speeches was not completed until the beginning of the Jewish Sabbath on a Friday afternoon.   An MK from the small ultraorthodox Poalei Agudat Yisrael (PAY) quickly tabled a motion of no-confidence against the government for desecrating the Sabbath.   The cabinet issued a statement formally expressing its regret that the Sabbath had been unintentionally violated.   The no-confidence motion was defeated.   But in the Knesset vote all but one of the NRP MKs abstained, jeopardizing the government's tenure.   For partners in a coalition government abstention in such a vote is tantamount to opposing the government and violates the law on

collective responsibility. Prime Minister Rabin
fired the three NRP ministers in the cabinet and
resigned as head of the government. A caretaker
cabinet was set up under Rabin until new elections
were held. Elections originally scheduled for the
fall were moved up to May 1977. Some Rabin critics charged that this shift indicated he was more
interested in keeping the opposition parties off-
balance than in safeguarding the principle of
collective responsibility. Few observers noted at
the time that the "historic alliance" between
Labor and the NRP was in the process of being
severed.

Concurrently with the cabinet crisis a rash of
scandals involving high government officials
erupted. Asher Yadlin, only recently nominated
for the prestigious post of head of the Bank of
Israel, was arrested and charged with gross financial misconduct during his term as director of the
Histadrut Sick Fund. In a highly publicized trial
Yadlin was convicted of bribery and sentenced to
five years' imprisonment. Early in January 1977
Housing Minister Avrahan Ofer, long a leading
figure in the Labor party, committed suicide. He
had been under investigation for his efforts to
raise money for the Labor party, while acting as
director of the Histadrut housing company. His
suicide was widely attributed to the tepid support
he had received from party colleagues, but Rabin
claimed Ofer was the victim of a sensationalist
press.

Defense Minister Shimon Peres, whom Rabin had
defeated for party leadership in 1974, decided to
contest Rabin's leadership in the pending election. In Rabin's memoirs Peres is castigated for
having repeatedly undermined cabinet unity by
publicly airing his difference with Rabin over
such policies as the size of the defense budget
and restriction of Jewish settlements on the West
Bank.(1) Rabin narrowly defeated Peres by a margin of 51 votes, and was confirmed in the No. 1
position on the Alignment's electoral list.

1. *The Rabin Memoirs*, Yitzhak Rabin (Boston: Little Brown, 1979),
p. 307.

Yet another scandal broke when several prominent persons were charged with violations of
foreign currency regulations, including Rabin's
wife, Leah, and former Foreign Minister Abba Eban.
Rabin himself decided to accept co-responsibility
with his wife for maintaining a joint U.S. bank
account after Rabin left his ambassadorial post in
Washington. Both Rabin and his wife were fined
for their offense. Rabin then took a leave of
absence until after the election and vacated his
top position on the Alignment list. By an overwhelming majority of the central committee Peres
was named party leader and became Labor's major
campaign spokesman.

The Labor government incurred two additional
blows prior to the election. The State Controller
issued a damaging report that current military
supplies in IDF emergency warehouses were inade-
quate. A week before the election a military
helicopter crashed with 54 soldiers on board.
Both these incidents reflected negatively on
Peres' position as Defense Minister. Never had
the Labor party entered an election so sorely
wounded.

(2) The Campaign

*New Challenger: the Democratic Movement for
Change*

In the aftermath of the Yom Kippur War public
dissatisfaction with the ruling Establishment--the
Labor/Histadrut complex, markedly increased and
led to the formation of several reformist groups.
The Democratic Movement for Change (DMC) was the
most important manifestation of this trend, becoming a serious contender in the 1977 election.

The DMC represented a fusion of two separately
organized groups. The first of these was *Shinui*
(Change) organized in 1974 by Professor Amnon

Rubinstein, former dean of Tel Aviv University law school. A year and a half later Yigael Yadin, noted archeologist and IDF chief of staff in Israel's War of Independence, launched his own group called the Democratic Movement. Rubinstein's group was comprised mostly of younger professionals. Yadin's organization attracted an older, high status group, including a number of persons holding key positions in the economy and several former chiefs of staff.

By merging each of the groupings made gains. In Yadin Shinui gained a senior leader of national stature, while Yadin's Democratic Movement was able to utilize the existing organizational apparatus of Rubinstein's group.(2) On the DMC electoral list Yadin held the No. 1 slot and Rubinstein the second position.

The DMC attracted support from diverse sources. Three of its prominent leaders had been previously associated with the Labor alignment: Meir Amit, head of an industrial conglomerate in Histadrut; Meir Zorea, head of the National Lands Authority; and Shmuel Toledano, former adviser to the Prime Minister on Arab affairs.(3) Led by M. K. Shmuel Tamir, the Free Center group, previously allied to the Likud bloc, transferred its allegiance to the DMC. Affiliation by the *Odet* group of Oriental Jews helped offset the DMC's image as an essentially Ashkenazim party.

As a reformist party the DMC's primary target was the incumbent Labor party, which in the DMC's view was controlled by entrenched factions preoccupied with maintaining the status quo. Electoral reform was made the centerpiece of the DMC platform. The party favored the division of the country into several districts to replace the single national constituency of the existing PR system. The DMC also called for opening up the elitist party nominating system to all party members and

2. "A Movement for Change in a Stable System," Efraim Torgovnik in Asher Arian's *The Elections in Israel--1977* (Jerusalem: Jerusalem Academic Press, 1980), p. 79.

3. Amit was assigned the number 3 slot on the DMC electoral list.

was itself the first party to introduce a direct primary for candidate selection.

The DMC was committed to "closing the social gap" between the privileged sector and large numbers of poor people by means of an expanded social welfare system, including a national health service. DMC spokesmen criticized Israel's lack of economic self-sufficiency, and called for reduced dependency on financial assistance from the United States.(4) The DMC also advocated the streamlining of Israel's overstaffed governmental bureaucracy by eliminating some ministries and combining others.

With its heterogenous support the DMC had difficulty in formulating its position on the territorial question. It ended up with a plank not dissimilar from Labor's: (1)approval for a Palestinian-Jordanian relationship but no Palestinian state on the West Bank; (2)exclusion of the PLO from peace negotiations; and (3)restricted Jewish settlements on the West Bank. This moderate stance was expected to attract some Labor voters to the DMC.

The Likud Campaign

The Likud bloc entered the campaign with improved prospects but with its leaders still uncertain that an electoral breakthrough was at hand. The primary objective of the party platform was to reconcile the divergent interests which Likud represented. On economic policy the Herut wing maintained a populist stance, intended to attract support from the working class, especially disadvantaged Oriental Jews. The Liberals, representing business groups like the Israel Manufacturers Association and agricultural smallholders, advocated a drastic reduction in the public sector of the economy and an enlarged private sector. The Liberals also were eager to curb the formidable economic power of the Histadrut with its close

4. Torgovnik, op. cit., p 86.

ties to past Labor governments. On foreign policy and security issues the Herut held a militantly nationalist position, which won enthusiastic support from many Oriental Jews, while a number of Liberals favored at least limited concessions on the territorial question. With some qualifications the Likud's economic platform tended to reflect Liberal preferences, the foreign policy planks those of Herut.

In Likud's economic platform inflation was called "the number one enemy of the people." Likud promised to reduce it by half, to 15 percent within a year and then to ten percent.(5) Within five years the GNP was to be increased 40 percent by encouraging private investment, introducing new productivity schemes and promoting worker mobility. Likud also promised to sell public corporations, cease public construction of housing and nationalize the health services.

On security issues the Likud platform reiterated Israel's claim to Judea and Samaria (i.e. the West Bank) as well as Gaza, and the need for "secure and defensible" boundaries in the Sinai and Golan. Israel's right to make Jewish settlement in all parts of Eretz Israel was reasserted. Arabs who promised loyalty to Israel would be granted equal rights. In peace negotiations a Likud government would enter into direct "face-to-face" negotiations with the Arabs with "no prior conditions" and with each side "free to advance proposals."(6) Likud's position stood in sharp contrast to Labor's willingness to make territorial concessions in a future peace settlement and entertain the alternative of a Palestinian-Jordanian state.

On the questions of religion the Likud platform stressed both adherence to religious tradition, which pleased Herut supporters, and individual freedom of conscience, a traditional Liberal concern. To combat the alleged "value-neutral approach" in the Israeli educational system, Likud

5. The 1977 platform of the Likud.

6. Ibid.

proposed an active inculcation of "Jewish con-
sciousness and Zionism."

The management of the campaign was entrusted to
Ezer Weizman, one-time commander of the Israeli
Air Force, who had joined Herut in 1969. With
Menachem Begin immobilized by a heart attack,
Weizman's campaign staff assumed active control.
Use of television became an especially important
campaign tactic. Prime time on television was
allocated on the basis of the relative strength of
the parties in the outgoing Knesset. This proved
advantageous to Likud as the second largest party.
Weizman hired a commercial public relations firm
to plan Likud's media effort. In most of its TV
spots Likud ignored the lesser parties and concentrated its fire on the beleaguered Labor alignment. Likud depicted the outgoing Labor government as riddled with corruption, condemned the
current high rate of inflation and criticized its
ineffectualness in dealing with a rash of labor
disputes. When Begin recovered near the end of
the campaign, he engaged in an hour-long debate on
television with Labor's Shimon Peres, which was
widely regarded as having given the Likud campaign
an important boost.

The NRP Turns Right

The NRP's exclusion from the Rabin government
enabled it to run its election campaign as an
opposition party. Before the NRP set its campaign
strategy, resolution of its ongoing factional
struggles was attempted.

The NRP was considered the most factionalized
Israeli party. In the 1970s seven factions competed in its internal elections. Since no faction
won a majority, the party was governed by a shifting coalition of factions.(7) These were formed

7. "Factionalism in the National Religious Party: The Quiet Revolution," Yael Yishai in Arian (1977 Election), p. 58. Yishai de-
fines a party faction "as a group of party members, operating
within the framework of the parent party, organized for the purpose of replacing the party's policies or leadership."

on the basis of divisions over controversial issues, especially national security questions, and personality clashes among factional leaders. On the eve of the 1977 election three factions played a critically important role: (1)the *Likud Utmura* faction, led by Yitzhak Raphael, a Knesset member since 1952 and Minister of Religious Affairs in Prime Minister Rabin's cabinet; (2)the *Lamifne* faction, headed by the long-time party leader, Dr. Yosef Burg; and (3)the "Young Guard" faction, led by Zevulun Hammer and Yehuda Ben-Meir, intent on replacing NRP's traditional leaders.

The Young Guard faction emerged in a period of radical social change in Israel's religious community, beginning in the 1950s. Two aspects were especially noteworthy: (1)the increasingly important role of yeshiva high schools in the religious educational "stream," with their marked emphasis on Talmudic studies and strict religious observances; and (2)the process of "ghettoization"--the recent tendency of segments of the religious population to live by conscious choice in special residential areas.(8) Both developments were a response by deeply pious Jews to the perceived threat of "creeping secularism." In its early stage the Young Guard functioned primarily as an organization to provide leisure-time activities for religious young people. It entered active NRP politics with the clear intent of taking over party leadership and moving the NRP decisively to the right on the issue of Greater Israel.

The Young Guard formed close relations with Gush Emunim, whose militantly nationalist views it shared. It unsuccessfully attempted to prevent the NRP's reentry in Rabin's cabinet in October 1974 because of its dovish position on partial withdrawal from the occupied territories, which the Raphael and Burg factions supported. At one point Hammer and Ben-Meir considered defecting from the NRP, and carried out preliminary negotia-

8. "The NRP in Transition--Behind the Party's Electoral Decline," Menahem Friedman in *The Roots of Begin's Success,* edited by Caspi, Diskin, and Gutmann (London and Canberra: Croom Helm, 1984), pp. 152-57.

tions with Gush Emunim on forming a new party. In the end they adhered to their original objective of taking over the NRP from within.

As a first step the Young Guard sought the removal of Raphael from party leadership. Raphael's political career had been marred by several scandals. In 1965 when he was deputy Minister of Health, Raphael was accused of helping to bribe a senior civil servant. Although acquitted for lack of evidence, a state commission of inquiry later rendered a negative report against him. In 1974 Raphael was regarded as chiefly responsible for NRP's reentry in the Rabin government in order to advance his own ministerial ambitions. In December 1976 after pretending to accept Prime Minister Rabin's apologies for the F-15 incident, Raphael refused to support the government in the crucial no-confidence vote.(9)

The Young Guard's strategy was to break the long-standing alliance between Raphael's Likud Utmura faction and Burg's Lamifne faction, build a new factional coalition and isolate Raphael in NRP's internal election prior to the 1977 Knesset election. The Young Guard first aligned itself with the small Central faction, led by Zerah War-haftig. These two groups then joined with a new party faction called the Movement for National Political Revival(NRV) comprised of religious intellectuals and West Bank settlers. The NRV faction, holding extreme hardline views on Greater Israel, insisted the NRP leadership be reorganized on a "spiritual" basis, or otherwise the NRV faction would withdraw from the party. In its campaign the NRV advanced the slogan--"a more beautiful NRP," which implied an NRP without Raphael.

Lamifne's leader, Yosef Burg, was in an increasingly untenable position, caught between the rapidly growing NRV faction and Raphael's faction, his former ally. As a member of Rabin's cabinet Burg had been miffed by Raphael's use of his ministerial position to channel government patronage to his own faction. After the forced

9. Yishai, op. cit., p. 66.

resignation of NRP's ministers from Rabin's cabinet, Burg's Lamifne faction voted to ally with NRV and in effect with the Young Guard. This new factional coalition was joined by two other factions--the religious moshavim and kibbutzim factions. The new bloc controlled nearly 75 percent of the party vote.

Raphael's position was further weakened by opposition from two of his own faction's younger leaders--David Glass, director general of the Ministry of Religious Affairs, and Aharon Abuhatzeira, mayor of Ramla, and a prominent leader of North African Jews. Unwilling to risk their political careers, Glass and Abuhatzeira strongly opposed Raphael's effort to withdraw his Likud Utmura faction from the NRP and set up a new splinter party.

In the party election held in March 1977 to choose factional representatives on the NRP's Knesset list, the Likud Utmura faction was assigned three positions. In the election Raphael came in fourth, and for the first time in his political career, was left off the NRP's electoral list.

The Young Guard's victory over Raphael was reinforced, when Rabbi Haim Druckman, a leading figure in Gush Emunim circles, was assigned the No. 2 position on the NRP list. In the 1977 campaign the new NRP leadership indicated that if its post-election options were between coalition with Labor or Likud, the NRP would opt for Likud.

Renovating Nomination Procedures

In 1977 several political parties attempted to decentralize and democratize their nomination procedures in Knesset elections. The use of the secret ballot by larger nominating bodies than in previous elections was the favored method of reform. The changes introduced by the DMC, the Herut and Labor will be briefly summarized.

The most radical innovation was the direct

primary election instituted by the DMC.(10) All
the approximately 35,000 members of the party were
eligible to vote and be nominated for DMC's electoral list. A prospective DMC member had only to
enroll and pay a membership fee. In advance of
the primary candidates publicized their programs
in a party booklet and in meetings held in urban
centers. About 80 percent of DMC members voted in
the party primary.

It produced an oddly unbalanced list, there
being only one Oriental Jew and no women among the
first 15 places (the DMZ subsequently won 15 seats
in the election). Two members of the small Druze
minority won "safe" seats, indicating that a
small, organized group could get a candidate ad-
vantageously placed. Three of the first 10 places
were won by the Free Center previously associated
with the Likud, while Shinui, one of the two DMC
founders, won only two out of the first 10 places.
Heavy pressure was placed on DMC leader Yadin to
amend the results, especially to assign Oriental
Jews more safe seats, but to no avail. Outside
the party the DMC primary was criticized as a
"lottery" and "a tribal democracy which does not
exist even in Saudi Arabia."

In the Likud bloc the three member parties--
Herut, the Liberals and La'am--were assigned
places on the combined bloc list according to a
previously negotiated agreement. Each of the
three parties was responsbile for naming and rank-
ordering its own Knesset candidates. The Herut,
which had used a small nominating committee in the
1973 election, adopted a complicated new system
which appreciably widened membership participation.(11) Herut's central committee was enlarged
to 640 members, giving the party branches more
representation. The party's electoral list was
chosen by secret ballot in a sequence of five

10. "Democracy and Representation in Israeli Political Parties,"
Giora Goldberg in Arian (1977 Election), pp. 103-4.

11. "Candidate Selection in Israel's Parliament: The Realities of
Change," Steven A. Hoffman, *Middle East Journal* 34, no. 3 (1980):
292-95.

votes. A single balloting was held to decide who would be first on the Herut list (and hence on the Likud list), a position easily won by Menachem Begin. The central committee then named 35 candidates in a series of voting rounds. Each round placed seven candidates in succession on the party list. Critics of the Herut's system charged that voting in separate stages encouraged manipulation by party leaders. Some critics claimed that Begin himself could determine the first seven or eight positions. Other observers claimed that some local branch leaders exerted significant influence in candidate selection.

The top four positions on the combined Likud list were assigned to the Herut's Begin; Simcha Ehrlich, Liberal party chairman; Yigal Hurvitz, representing the small La´am party; and Ezer Weizman of Herut. Likud attempted unsuccessfully to persuade Moshe Dayan to desert the Labor alignment and accept a safe seat on its list. In the first ten Likud positions Herut was assigned the No. 1, 4, 6 and 8 positions; the Liberals Nos. 2, 5, 7 and 9; and La´am No. 3 and 10. Many observers believed that Herut was underrepresented in number of safe seats, and the Liberals and La´am parties were overrepresented.

The Labor party made two important changes in its nominating procedure.(12) First, the principle of rotation was adopted. The party convention decided that Labor MKs who had served in the Knesset for eight years or more would require the support of at least 60 percent of its 800-member central committee in a secret ballot vote. Seven of 17 veteran MKs failed to gain the necessary majority. Secondly 20 percent of the places on the party list were reserved for women, and 40 percent were allocated to party branches.

But a small nominating committee of seven members retained a decisive voice. The committee reflected the major factional divisions in the party: two were from Peres´ camp, two from Rabin´s camp, two neutrals and an additional repre-

12. Goldberg, op. cit., pp. 109-10.

sentative of the women's sector. Most nominees
from the party branches and the women's sector
failed to gain "realistic" places, leaving the
allocation of most safe seats to the party center. After Rabin's resignation, the new party
leader, Peres, made a special agreement with
Foreign Minister Yigal Allon, which provided that
Peres would take the No. 1 slot and Allon, No. 2.
Allon was also promised the Defense Ministry in
the next Labor government. Once the nominating
committee completed the party list, it was approved en bloc by the central committee.

TABLE I

1977 Election Results

Party	Votes	%	Knesset Seats
Likud	583,075	33.4	43
Labor Alignment	430,023	24.6	32
Democratic Movement for Change	202,265	11.6	15
National Religious Party	160,787	9.2	12
Democratic Front	79,733	4.6	5
Agudat Yisrael	58,652	3.4	4
Flatto-Sharon	35,049	2.0	1
Shlomzion (Sharon)	33,947	1.9	2
Shelli	27,281	1.6	2
United Arab List	24,185	1.4	1
Poalei Agudat Yisrael	23,956	1.4	1
Independent Liberal	21,277	1.2	1
Citizens Rights Movements	20,621	1.2	1
Others	46,969	2.7	0
Total	1,747,820	100.0	120

(3) Election Results

The most important results of the 1977 election
were the drastic slippage in the Labor alignment
vote, the impressive first-time showing of the DMC
and Likud's winning the largest number of Knesset
seats. Labor's popular vote dropped from 39.6
percent in 1973 to an all-time low of 24.6 percent
in 1977, and its Knesset representation decreased
from 51 to 32 seats. Begin's Likud won 33.4
percent of the popular vote and won 43 seats, four
more than in 1973. Yadin's DMC made a highly
creditable first showing with 11.6 percent of the
vote and 15 seats. In fourth place the NRP got
9.2 percent of the vote and 12 seats, an increase
of two. Nine lesser parties won 18.7 percent of
the vote and shared 18 seats. Nine other parties
failed to win the one percent of the vote required
for Knesset representation. As in most Knesset
elections, the turnout was high--79.2 percent of
the electorate--compared to 78.6 in 1973. (See
Table I)

Labor's poor showing meant that after 29 years,
it could no longer form a government. The Likud
was now enabled to move from its perennial position as leader of the opposition to an unwonted
role of governing party. Many observers had moni-
tored Labor's gradual decline and expected the
emergence of an alternative government in the near
future. In each of the three previous elections
the Labor plurality had decreased. But the pre-
election polls in 1977 produced mixed results.
The March polls gave the Alignment a slight edge,
in April Labor and Likud were running even and in
the final poll two weeks before the election on
May 17, Likud held a narrow lead. But the surprising size of the undecided vote--34 percent,
introduced an element of unpredictabliity in electoral expectations.

Labor Defections

The election results were widely interpreted as a sweeping rejection of the Labor alignment rather than a positive endorsement of a Likud government. The marked shift away from Labor was unevenly divided between Likud and the DMC.(13) The effect was to diminish the broad base of voter support that Labor had long enjoyed. Upper-middle class Ashkenazim voters with high levels of education moved in large numbers to the DMC. Many lower-class workers with an Asia-African background joined their fellow Oriental Jews who already constituted a major Likud constituency.

This differential pattern was reflected in the voting results in established cities compared to those in the newer development towns. In cities established before 1948, Labor's vote dropped an astonishing 15.8 percent, from 39.7 percent in the 1973 election to 23.9 percent in 1977. The DMC received an impressive 13.7 percent of this urban vote. The Likud made only a four percent gain in these older cities. In cities established after 1948--many of them development towns with a large Oriental population, the slippage in the Labor vote was even more marked--from 40.4 percent in 1973 to 23 percent in 1977. The Likud was the chief beneficiary of this shift, increasing its 1973 vote from 32.6 percent to 44 percent in 1977. But the DMC was able to win 7.2 percent of the vote in the newer cities.(14)

Even in the kibbutz movement, long a Labor stronghold, the Alignment vote dropped some ten percentage points with the DMC as the chief beneficiary. In the *Ihud* kibbutz federation, with past ties to Mapai and a powerful force in the Labor party, there was an interesting differential. In the kibbutzim established before 1948, the Labor vote dropped from 89.4 percent in 1973

13. See Asher Arian's article, "The Electorate: Israel 1977," for a detailed analysis of election results, in Penniman, op. cit., pp. 59-89.

14. Ibid., p. 63.

to 72.3 percent in 1977, most of this vote going to DMC. In kibbutzim founded after 1948, the Alignment vote decreased by twenty percentage points, of which the DMC won 18.8 percent. Interestingly the drop in the Labor vote in the Mapam-affiliated kibbutzim was significantly lower. In this case more defectors opted for a small leftist party (Shelli) than for the DMC.

In summary the DMC tended to gain the highly educated, upper-income Labor defectors of European background, while most Labor defectors to the Likud were Oriental working-class voters.

An Increase in the "Floating Vote"

A significant feature of recent Knesset elections has been the progressively increasing size of the floating vote--that is, those voters that shift their party preferences between elections. Arian's research indicates that between the 1965 and 1969 elections about a quarter of the population changed its vote, and between 1969 and 1973 about a third. In 1977 half the electorate changed its vote.(15) Of the 44.5 percent in the research sample who voted for the Alignment in 1973, less than half did so in 1977, with 20 percent going to the Likud and 18 percent to the DMC. The 1973 Likud voters remained mostly loyal, although some eight percent voted for the DMC in 1977.

The Contrasting Labor and Likud Electorates

The significant differentials between the electorates of the two leading parties are age, ethnicity and levels of education and income. In part these differentials reflect the historic position of the Labor party--its association with independence and the full range of government policies in Israel's nation-building phase, the traditional

15. Ibid., p. 65.

opposition role of the Likud and the dove-hawk
cleavage between Labor and Likud. Since the late
1960s Labor has increasingly relied on a conservative electorate: the elderly more than the young,
women more than men, and the middle education and
income levels.(16)

The loss of Labor support in the youngest voting group (24 and less) is especially striking.
Between the 1973 and 1977 elections Labor's support in this age group dropped from 39 to 20
percent, while the Likud's percentage increased
from 44 to 51 percent. The DMC was the major
beneficiary of this shift in 1977, drawing 21
percent of the youngest voters. In the oldest
voting group (50 and above) the Alignment has
consistently attracted more than half, while the
Likud in 1977, as in the 1969 and 1973, received
about a third.

In the critically important group of immigrant
voters Arian's research shows that Labor has been
especially successful among Jews who immigrated to
Israel before independence or immediately thereafter and those born in Europe and America, the
Ashkenazim. In the first generation after independence Labor also enjoyed substantial support
among Asian-African (Oriental) immigrants. In the
second generation the Likud began to make significant inroads among the Oriental Jews as well as
their children born in Israel *(sabras)*. In 1977
the Alignment had the support of nearly half the
European-American born, while Likud had less than
a fifth. Among Asian-African immigrants, however,
the Likud attracted 46 percent, Labor only 32
percent. Even more significantly, among native-
born Israelis with Asian-African fathers the Likud
received 65 percent of their vote, compared to 23
percent for Labor. Furthermore Likud attracted
the same percentage(23) of sabras born of Europe-
American fathers as did Labor. Since Oriental
families tend to have considerably more children
than Ashkenazis, Likud's present advantage in this
ethnic group is likely to increase. An important

16. Ibid., pp. 77-84.

64

political factor--Likud's more hawkish position on
Greater Israel, partly explains its special attraction to Orientals, most of whom previously
lived under harsh Arab regimes. Interestingly,
support for Likud among Israel-born voters who
have Asian-African fathers, tends to decrease as
their educational level increases. Since 1969
this better-educated group has tended to vote for
one of the smaller parties.

In Arian's study the 1977 election confirms a
recent trend toward class politics.(17) Traditionally the Labor party derived support from all
social strata, whereas much of Likud's support
came from a combination of lower-class voters
(Herut) and upper and middle class voters (Liberals), although more of these two groups voted
Labor. In 1977 many of Labor's middle class voters and those of Asian-African background shifted
to the Likud, while many sabras with Ashkenazim
parents and with more than a high school education
voted DMC. Whether Labor could recapture its
original broad base of support, especially among
working class Orientals, without an upheaval in
its party leadership, appeared doubtful.

The Lesser Parties

(1)*The religious parties*. Although it is estimated that Israel's orthodox population comprises
about a third of its total population, only between 13-15 percent of the electorate usually
votes for religious parties. Since the mid-1950s
there have been three religious parties of variable size: the largest is the NRP, which usually
held between 10 and 12 Knesset seats; and the much
smaller ultraorthodox parties, the Agudat Israel,
and its worker counterpart, Poalei Agudat Israel
(PAY). While the NRP was an invariable partner in
Labor coalition governments until 1977, the Agudat
regularly declined to participate in secular governments. The more flexible PAY took part in some

17. Ibid., pp. 85-88.

governments. The relationship between Agudat and PAY was uneven. In some years the two parties formed a Torah Religious Front and sponsored a common list; in other years they ran separately.

The 1977 results were variable for these three parties. The NRP improved its position, increasing its popular vote from 8.3 percent to 9.2 percent and winning two additional seats for a total of 12. Most of the NRP increase came from a pivotal "swing" group of younger, ideologically oriented, Israeli-born Ashkenazi. Most of these voters had defected to the Likud in 1973, but returned to the NRP fold in 1977 after the factional victory of the Young Guard. (18) During the campaign it became clear that a revitalized and more rightist NRP would respond affirmatively, if invited to join a new Likud coalition.

In the 1973 election the Agudat and PAY, united in the Torah Front, won five Knesset seats. Subsequently some members of PAY's youth movement were attracted to Gush Emunim, and in 1977 transferred their votes either to the Likud or the NRP, both more nationalistic than Poalei. In 1977 PAY lost one of its two seats, and received only 1.4 percent of the popular vote. The Agudat, which had rejected a unified list with PAY, retained its usual voter support and won four Knesset seats.

(2)*The special case of Sharon's Shlomzion list.* General Ariel Sharon represents the archtypical Israeli military hero turned politician. His brilliant military career extended over a period of more than 20 years. Sharon was in charge of reprisal actions against the Palestinians in 1954-56 and commanded the parachutists who launched the Sinai campaign in the 1956 war. In the Six-Day War he commanded a division, and during most of the War of Attrition with Egypt, headed the Southern Command. In the Yom Kippur War he initiated the daring Suez Canal crossing and rapid Israeli advance on Cairo.

In politics Sharon's role has been somewhat

18. *Religion and Politics in Israel,* Charles S. Liebman and Eliezer Don-Yehiya (Bloomington: Indiana University Press, 1984), p. 115.

quixotic and at times catalytic. In 1973 he
played a key role in the formation of the Likud
bloc. He first joined the Liberal party, affiliated with Begin's Herut party in the Gahal bloc.
Sharon proposed the creation of a larger center-
right party with improved chances of becoming an
alternative government. It included Tamir's Free
Center party and the State list now headed by
Yigal Hurwitz. Begin reportedly initially opposed
Sharon's proposal, fearing he might have to yield
his tight control over the relatively small Gahal,
especially if the fractious Tamir entered the
bloc. Ezer Weizman, who had virtually withdrawn
from Herut, was induced by Sharon to participate
in the new enlarged organization.(19)

Sharon was elected to the Knesset in 1973, but
shortly resigned his seat to keep his army reserve
appointment. Later he became special military
adviser to Prime Minister Rabin, an appointment
that infuriated Defense Minister Peres.

In 1977 Sharon reentered active politics.
First he tried to rejoin the Likud, but his scheme
to replace Begin as party leader failed. His
former allies in the Liberal party now opposed his
reentry. Ehrlich, the Liberal party leader,
claimed that Sharon, though an outstanding military leader, was "unfit for politics." The resourceful Sharon then formed his own personal
political grouping, which he called *Shlomzion*
(Peace for Zion) with policy positions similar to
Likud's. His party attracted persons holding high
academic and military positions, but many of them
later withdrew--strongly criticizing Sharon's al-
legedly undemocratic methods. In the election
Shlomzion won two Knesset seats. Shortly thereafter its two MKs united with the Herut party, and
it was clear Sharon would win a cabinet post.

(3)*Two leftist parties*. On the far left there
were two parties: (1)a new grouping called *Shelli*
(Peace for Israel), and (2)the established Communist list, *Rakah*.

19. "Likud 1977-81: The Consolidation of Power," Efraim Torgovnik,
in *Israel in the Begin Era*, ed. Robert O. Freedman (New York:
Praeger, 1982), p. 11.

Shelli represented a loose amalgamation of three dovish factions: (1)*Moked* (Focus), which included former members of one of the Jewish Communist parties *(Maki)* and assorted leftists; (2)the "New Power" faction, headed by Uri Avneri, editor of a sensational weekly, former MK and long-time dove; and (3)a remnant of the Black Panthers. Shelli's leader was Arieh Eliav, highly respected as one-time secretary-general of the Labor party and previously holder of two sub-cabinet posts. Shelli was supported by a number of left-wing intellectuals, who advocated closer relations between Israeli and Palestinian Arabs. Shelli hoped to draw votes from the leftist Mapam, affiliated with the Alignment, and from the left wing of the Labor party. But Shelli won only two Knesset seats. Eliav became its chief parliamentary spokesman.

Rakah. In the 1973 election Rakah had won four Knesset seats. Prior to the 1977 election Rakah expanded its activities in its major constituency, the Israeli Arabs. In March 1976 Rakah organized a country wide general strike among the Arabs to protest the government's land expropriation policy. Nearly 25 percent of Arab workers absented themselves from their jobs at Jewish farms, factories and construction sites. Troops were quickly dispatched to Arab areas, and for the first time there were armed clashes with Arab protesters, six Arabs being killed and 70 injured.[20] This dramatic event was hereafter called Land Day, symbol of Arab intransigence. Buoyed by its new prominence, Rakah won an absolute majority in the local council of Arab Nazareth.

In the 1977 election Rakah revived the electoral strategy of the popular front, hoping to enlarge its Knesset delegation. It formed an alliance with other leftist groups, which was called the Democratic Front for Peace and Equality (DFPE). It included a Black Panther faction, which increased its Jewish component. The election results proved disappointing to Rakah, when

20. Ibid., Israel's Arab Minority in the Begin Era" by Ian Lustick, p. 123.

it added only one seat to its Knesset delegation. Rakah could boast, however, that it had substantially increased its percentage of the critically important Arab vote--from 37 percent in 1973 to nearly half in 1977. In Arab settlements involved in Land Day demonstrations, Rakah's vote was particularly heavy. Of the DFPE's five Knesset seats, three were held by Arabs.

(4)*Other parties.* The *Independent Liberal party*(ILP), formed in 1965 as a splinter off the mainstream party, was virtually wiped out in 1977. Its Knesset representation was reduced from four to one seat. The ILP was heir to the Progressive party, which had united with the centrist General Zionists in 1961 to form the Liberal party. The ILP demurred from the Liberal party's union with Herut in 1965. After 1967 the ILP maintained a dovish position on the territorial question and was frequently a member of Labor coalitions. Its stunning loss in 1977 was mainly attributed to its close association with the discredited Rabin government and defection of many of its supporters to Yadin's reformist DMC.

The Movement for Citizens' Rights (CRM) was founded in 1973 by Shulamit Aloni, a controversial figure in Israeli politics since the early 1960s. As a maverick Labor MK, Aloni clashed with Prime Minister Golda Meir, especially over Aloni's criticism of Labor's concessions to the NRP on the "Who is a Jew?" question. In 1973 CRM won three seats, and in 1974 after Meir's resignation, Aloni joined the Rabin government as Minister without Portfolio. She resigned, however, when the NRP rejoined the government. In the 1977 campaign the CRM's main target was Yadin's DMC, which appealed to the same professional group as CRM. CRM attacked the vagueness of the DMC platform, especially on religious questions. The CRM's apprehension over DMC's voter appeal proved justified; it barely qualified (1.2 percent of the popular vote) for a single seat in the new Knesset.

(5)*Two mavericks.* Israeli politics are strongly party dominated, and few MKs have been elected as independents. The most unusual candidate competing in 1977 was Shmuel Flatto-Sharon, running on a one-man list. He was a wealthy Jew who had come to Israel in 1973, to avoid charges he faced in France regarding his financial affairs. If he were elected to the Knesset, he would enjoy immunity from extradition back to France. Despite his limited knowledge of Hebrew and lack of party connections, he made a favorable impression on the campaign trail, promising the development areas extensive largesse, if he were elected. He adopted the odd slogan, "the solitary man in the Knesset." He made a surprisingly good showing, winning 35,000 votes (slightly more than General Sharon), which was sufficient to qualify his list for two seats (had there been a second candidate).

In the nine electoral lists that were defeated, the most noteworthy was that of Rabbi Meir Kahane, founder of the notorious Jewish Defense League in New York. After immigrating to Israel, Kahane became identified with the most extreme anti-Arab position, advocating a policy of obligatory Arab emigration out of Israel. In his 1973 campaign he nearly won a seat. In 1977 his *Kach* list got only about 4,000 votes (0.25 percent of the popular vote), and its future was uncertain.

The Arab Vote

In 1977 the most significant aspect of the Arab vote was the high percentage (nearly half) won by the Communist Rakah. As in previous elections the Labor alignment used the device of the affiliated Arab list, this time by uniting its two traditional Arab lists in a single list. Labor suffered a serious setback with Arab voters. Only one candidate on its single Arab list won a Knesset seat, compared to the three seats won by its two lists in 1973. The Arab vote for Labor combined with its Arab list constituted 27 percent of its vote.

While most of the votes lost by Labor's Arab list were transferred to Rakah, some went to a

protest list, organized by Mahmud Abbasi, onetime
activist in the Labor party. Abbasi criticized
Labor's practice of recruiting traditional Arab
leaders for its lists and ignoring younger, more
progressive Arab leadership. Abbasi's list received less than 6,000 votes, but these would have
sufficed to give Labor's Arab list a second Knesset seat. Despite efforts by Eliav's Shelli party
to attract Arab votes--including an overture to
the PLO, it won only one percent of the Arab vote.
The orthodox Jewish NRP got five percent of the
Arab vote, which was mainly attributed to the
NRP's past hold on patronage connected with the
Ministry of Religious Affairs.

For the first time the rate of Arab turnout
fell below that of the Jewish electorate to 74
percent. Political apathy was widespread in the
Arab population, while radical young Arabs undergoing "Palestinianization" were disinclined to
support any Zionist party.

The Histadrut Elections

In Israel Histadrut elections are accorded
great importance, second only to parliamentary
elections. Until 1977 they preceded those for the
Knesset, and thus provided an early indication of
electoral trends. If they reflected a diminished
vote for Labor, its leaders had time to modify
party strategy for the Knesset elections. Through
a strategic miscalculation by the Labor leadership
in 1977, the Histadrut elections were set for
September, four months after the Knesset election.
Some observers argue that if the usual sequence
had been preserved in 1977, Labor's losses would
have been considerably reduced.

Stung by its devastating setback in the Knesset
polling, Labor mobilized all its forces for the
Histadrut election. The Histadrut's membership of
approximately 1.3 million is charged with choosing
delegates to the organization's convention (in
1977, the 13th), who in turn select its executive
officials. As in the case of the Knesset, Labor

had consistently won the largest plurality in all previous Histadrut elections. In 1973 the Alignment gained over 58 percent of the Histadrut vote. In 1977 there was a total of 11 lists, representing all the major political parties, except the religious ones, who had their own religious labor federations. Yadin headed a DMC list. Likud's list was headed by David Levy, an immigrant from Morocco, who had risen rapidly in the party's leadership ranks.

Labor's campaign, as in the Knesset election, relied heavily on kibbutzim personnel, who were dispatched to canvas neighboring development towns. Former Premier Golda Meir led a mass march in Tel Aviv. Labor spokesmen stressed the importance of continued Labor control of the Histadrut as a counterweight to a Likud-dominated government. For its part Likud asked Histadrut voters to reinforce Likud's victory in the parliamentary vote. Likud campaigners referred contemptuously to Labor's leaders as "Yadlin's associates," who were tainted by his financial scandals.

Over 900,000 Histadrut members (69 percent) voted. Labor's vote dropped less than originally anticipated--only three percent less than in 1973. Labor in fact received about 60,000 more votes than it had in the May Knesset election. Likud improved its Histadrut standing, by winning 28.1 percent of the popular vote, compared to 22.6 percent in 1973. But the Alignment won 55 percent of the popular vote and 841 delegates (over 400 more than Likud), which enabled Labor to retain firm control over Histadrut and retrieve some of its diminished prestige.

(4) Summary

Nearly all observers viewed the 1977 election as a turning point in Israeli politics. The following appear to be its major features:

The termination of the Labor party's dominance. Some Israeli political scientists have applied Duverger's concept of "dominant party" to Israeli politics. According to Duverger, a dominant party is one whose "doctrine, ideas, its style, so to speak, coincide with those (of a specific) epoch....Domination is a question of influence rather than of strength....A dominant party is that which public opinion believes to be dominant."(21) Duverger also links the collapse of a dominant party to a proportional electoral system (like Israel's), when the dominant party's loss means that a substantial number of voters transfer their support to other parties. One defeat, it is argued, is sufficient to bring domination to an end. The Israeli Labor party is historically identified with the era of independence and the formative phase of nation-building. In 1977 Labor lost more than a third of its voters, mainly to the DMC and the Likud.

A distinction is drawn between the immediate causes for Labor's decline and longer term ones. The former includes the final crisis of the Rabin government, the series of scandals, the aura of corruption. The underlying causes of its decline are extremely complex. Certain landmark events can be cited: the internal factional upheaval of the 1960s, climaxed by David Ben-Gurion's formation of a dissident party, the Rafi; Mapai's loss of monopoly control over ministerial assignments in the unity government at the time of the Six-Day War; the loss of public confidence in the Meir

---

21. Maurice Duverger, *Political Parties: Their Organization and Activity in the Modern State* (New York: Wiley, 1961), pp. 308-12. Israeli political scientists who employ Duverger's concept include Arian and Y. Shapiro. Other dominant party systems include the Nehru/Gandhi Congress Party in India and the Liberal Democratic Party in Japan.

government in the Yom Kippur War; the gradual
loss of Labor support in critical voting groups
such as the younger age groups and working-class
Oriental Jews; and the prolonged power struggle
between Rabin and Peres for Labor party leadership. A profound spiritual malaise appeared to
have overtaken the reigning Labor party.

  *Likud's legitimation as an alternative
government to Labor.* A key element in the
"dominant party" concept is the presence of an
ineffectual, fragmented opposition that is incapa-
ble of providing an effective alternative government. In Israel there was the special factor of
extremist parties on both the far left and extreme
right that had no plausible basis for uniting to
oppose the dominant party--the Communists on the
left and the Herut on the right. For three decades the symbolic figure in the opposition was
Menachem Begin with pariah status assigned him by
Ben-Gurion in 1947. Several factors combined to
legitimate the Begin party: its participation in
the national unity government (1967-70); the ideological polarization in Israeli politics, induced
by the dove-hawk controversy over the occupied
territories after 1967; the formation of a larger,
more supple rightist bloc, the Likud, in 1973; and
the shift to the right on the Greater Israel issue
in the NRP, which provided Begin with a cooperative ally to form an alternative government in
1977.

  *The emergence of a serious challenger to the
two established parties, the DMC.* In 1977 the
electorate was confronted with a unique situation:
three parties competing for power. For the first
time the voters were presented with more than one
real candidate for prime minister: Peres, Begin
or Yadin. When a large number of the Israeli
elite--former generals, corporate directors, high
government officals, university professors and
lawyers, flocked to the ranks of the DMC, speculation was rife that an unprecedented "Third Force"
had emerged. In retrospect the major functions of
the DMC appear to have been threefold: serving as

the chief vehicle for transfer of labor votes, insuring the end of Labor´s long dominance and expanding the parliamentary base of the new Begin government. After its impressive electoral showing and entry into the cabinet in 1977 the DMC was subject to fierce centrifugal pressure, lost its Shinui component and was defunct by the time of the 1981 election.

Primacy of domestic issues. In Israel, internal problems--the state of the economy, the extent of corruption in government, religious questions, compete with foreign policy and the chronic question of national security for voter attention. In 1977 polling data indicated that internal problems and a wide-spread desire for change were dominant. A pre-election poll in March on the most pressing current problem reported that for 37 percent, it was the economy; 27 percent, security; 13 percent, the social gap between rich and poor; and 9 percent, peace.(22) Interestingly, Alignment voters rated security over the economy as the nation´s most important problem. The May poll two weeks before the election confirmed the findings in March. But even in elections where security issues are not the main staple of campaign debate, they are present in the background and exert a subtle influence. In 1977, however, there were no major foreign policy developments to distract the voter.

The electorate moves right. There were several significant indications in the 1977 election that the Israeli electorate´s views on the future of the occupied territories were increasingly rightist: 1)both Likud´s larger plurality over 1973 and its increased support from hawkish Oriental voters; 2)the improved showing of the NRP, led by the hawkish Young Guard; and 3)the relatively poor showing of the most dovish parties, like the CRM, Shelli and the ILP. This rightist trend was confirmed by polling data gathered both before and immediately after the Knesset election. More than 40 percent of the sample wanted to return none of

22. Arian's article in Penniman, op. cit., p. 74.

the West Bank territory, more than a fifth only a small part. Only about 14 percent wanted to return "all" or "almost all" of the West Bank.(23) The most hawkish answers in the polls came predictably from the Likud (82 percent), but also a substantial 57 percent of Alignment voters. The overall rightist trend facilitated voter acceptance of the Likud as an appropriate alternative government.

Attentuated personality factor. In a small, highly literate and well-informed electorate like Israel´s, voters are sensitive to personal qualities of politicians who head the party lists. In 1977 there were two factors which reduced the importance of the personality factor. One was the fortuitous factor of Menachem Begin´s illness during most of the campaign, which placed the major burden of campaign operations on Likud professionals. The second was the chaotic situation in the Labor party leadership, where Rabin remained the titular head, and Peres was the chief front-line campaigner.

The trend toward generals-in-politics. As the major parties were increasingly confronted with leadership succession problems after the mid-1960s, there was active recruitment of retired military officers. The 1977 election confirmed the trend away from the older veteran politicians of the prestate period toward the wider use of military professionals. In the top leadership of the Labor party Rabin, Allon and Dayan had all had distinguished military careers. In the Likud there were Sharon and Weizman, and in the DMC, Yadin.

While most observers agreed that the single most important aspect of the 1977 election was the end of Labor´s dominance, there was active debate over the future shape of Israeli politics. Would the victorious Likud emerge as the new dominant party with further erosion of Labor party support? Or would a truly competitive system replace the obsolete dominant party system? If so, would a

23. Ibid., p 72.

stalemate emerge between the two leading parties with roughly even electoral support? Or would a new, unforseen political balance develop? Clearly several elections would be required for clarification of the future shape of the party system.

(5) Coalition Formation

As in previous elections no party or bloc in the 1977 election received the minimal number of seats (61) to insure control of the Knesset. The Likud won 43 seats to which the two seats of Sharon's party were immediately added. For the additional 18 seats which Likud required to form a viable government, MKs from the religious parties and Yadin's DMC appeared the likeliest prospects.

The Fundamental Law sets the formal framework for the sequence of steps prescribed for setting up a new government.(24) Under Article 6 the President is enjoined to initiate consultations with Knesset groups as soon as official election results are published. By established practice the President customarily conducts talks with all the Knesset groups to ascertain the MK likeliest to succeed in forming a new government. Once the President designates a particular party leader-- almost always the head of the largest party, he is given an initial period of 21 days to complete his task. At presidential discretion the prospective Prime Minister can be granted a second 21 days, if his first efforts proved unavailing. Subsequently the President can name other MKs to attempt fresh efforts. Knesset intervention is possible at the end of the first 21-day period when parliamentary groups can send the President a written request to name their choice of MK as organizer of a new cabinet. Should these various options be exhausted, the President is obliged to inform the Speaker of the Knesset there is no possibility of forming a government.

24. *Israel's Parliament: The Law of the Knesset,* Eliahus S. Likhouski (London: Oxford, 1971), p. 166.

The scope of the process of coalition formation is broad. The negotiating parties have to decide on allocation of ministerial portfolios among themselves and the detailed provisions of the Coalition Agreement. This document spells out future governmental policies the new cabinet will attempt to implement. The process is also likely to include distribution of deputy ministerial posts and assignment of committee chairmen in the Knesset. It extends over a considerable period of time varying from five to eight weeks. In 1955 eleven weeks of negotiation were required. At the end of the process the Knesset must approve the personnel of the new cabinet as well as the Coalition Agreement before the new government takes office.

These formal procedures are modified by established practice. In most cases the leader of the largest party following an election will already have held extensive conversations with his prospective coalition partners before he has been formally nominated by the President. This preliminary maneuvering, however important, does not preclude prolonged and difficult negotiations, once the President has acted.

Under Israel's dominant party system (1948-77) the process of coalition formation followed a distinctive pattern. Since no government could be formed without the dominant party, Mapai/Labor was in a strong position to maximize its share of the most significant "pay-offs" (ministerial positions) and allocate secondary "pay-offs" (less important positions) to minor coalition partners. Mapai/Labor consistently held an absolute majority in the cabinet, and controlled the key ministries (see Chapter 1). Minor parties had a limited option--join the coalition and receive minor pay-offs or remain in the opposition and risk obscurity. Mapai/Labor favored the largest possible coalitions, because the individual minor parties would then have less room to maneuver and extract concessions from the dominant party.(25) In 1977

25. "Coalition Politics in Israel," David Nachmias, *Comparative Political Studies* 7, no. 3 (1974): 316-33.

it was uncertain to what extent Begin's Likud, not yet acknowledged as a new dominant party, could follow the previous pattern.

President Katzir formally entrusted Begin with the task of forming a government on June 7. His negotiations were completed in two phases: (1)a relatively brief period of intense negotiations with the two religious parties, the NRP and Agudat, which enabled Begin to submit a cabinet list in a little over a month; and (2)a more extended phase of negotiations with Yadin's DMC, which led to an enlarged Begin cabinet with DMC representation.

The Dayan Appointment

Begin's unilateral decision to appoint Moshe Dayan, a member of the Labor opposition and controversial public figure, to the key post of Foreign Minister provoked heavy criticism. Dayan had been associated with the discredited Meir government in the Yom Kippur War. Both the Liberals, Begin's partners in the Likud, and Yadin's DMC had their own favored nominee, and were incensed by Begin's failure to consult them in advance. Dayan's Labor party colleagues denounced him for his "act of treachery" in joining Likud, insisted that he give up his seat in the Knesset and resign from the party. War widows and parents bereaved in the '73 war joined in protest; a thousand persons demonstrated outside Herut headquarters in Tel Aviv. Dayan resigned from the Labor party, but retained his Knesset seat as an independent.

The chief rationale for his appointment was that with Dayan as Foreign Minister, the Likud would support a slightly softer line on the territorial question. Dayan had presumably influenced a statement by Begin that as Prime Minister, he would not take any unilateral step to make the West Bank and Gaza a formal part of Israel (i.e. annex them). Dayan was also considered an asset in representing Israel in pending discussions on a Middle East peace settlement with President Carter

in Washington. Begin attempted to placate his
critics by promising the full cabinet list would
be subject to approval by all the coalition parties, once it was formed.

Negotiations with the Religious Parties

Begin's negotiations with the religious parties
were completed within a few weeks. When his negotiations with the DMC threatened to end in an
impasse, an accommodation with the demands of the
religious parties became urgent. The new leadership of the NRP held views on Greater Israel
similar to those of Begin, and strongly favored
entering a Likud-based coalition. For coalition
pay-offs, the NRP leaders hoped to retain the
three ministries held under Labor, and add the
powerful Ministry of Education.

In a significant departure from past practice,
the ultraorthodox Agudat was authorized by its
governing body, the Council of Torah Sages, a
prestigious group of senior rabbis, to join a
Likud government, although it was instructed not
to accept cabinet posts. In exchange for support-
ing Begin's nationalistic policies, the Agudat,
controlling four votes in the Knesset, was able to
extract important concessions on religious questions from the Likud.

Most importantly, the Agudat received assur-
ances that a Likud government would modify existing procedures for orthodox religious women
claiming exemption from service in the armed
forces. Instead of the required critical scrutiny
of their exemption requests by a review board, in
the future only a notarized statement as to the
applicant's religious commitment would be required.(26)

The Agudat also succeeded in securing pledges
from Begin for a substantial increase in the
State's financial support for its separate educa-

26. In 1978 the number of religious women exempted from military
service increased by a third.

tional system. In the large families that typify
the ultrorthodox community, there is a marked
tendency for some family members to engage in
prolonged, full-time study as adults.

Other concessions which Begin made the religious parties included: (1)enactment of a law to
tighten observance of the Jewish Sabbath, so there
would be practically no exceptions to closing of
businesses; (2)a change in the abortion law to
restrict the criteria for authorizing abortions by
the Ministry of Health, and (3)a prohibition of
postmortems without the family's consent in writ-
ing (Jewish law forbids operations on dead
bodies.) Begin also undertook to make "every effort" to secure a parliamentary majority for a
private member's bill that would sanction only
conversions made in accordance with Jewish rabbinical law *(halacha)* as the basis for official
registrations under the Law of Return.   Thirty-
five of the 43 clauses in the multiparty Coalition
Agreement submitted to the Knesset dealt with
religious questions.

The New Likud Cabinet

On June 20 a new 13-member Likud cabinet was
approved by the Knesset in a 63-53 vote, two more
than the minimal requirement. The Government's
majority was comprised of 45 Likud votes, 12 NRP,
four Agudat and the votes of two independents--
Moshe Dayan and the controversial newcomer,
Flatto-Sharon. The NRP fared well in the cabinet
assignments. Zevulun Hammer, the Young Guard
leader, won the coveted post of Minister of Education and Culture, which has jurisdiction over not
only the educational system but also broadcasting
and State support for the arts. Yosef Burg retained the Ministry of Interior, with which the
powerful Police Department was combined. The
fast-rising Moroccan politician, Aharon Abuhatzeira, was assigned the important Ministry of Religious Affairs. Within the Likud bloc the Herut

received four cabinet seats, the Liberals three and La'am two. The key posts held by the Herut were the office of Prime Minister (Begin), Defense Minister (Weizman) and Agriculture (Sharon). Herut's David Levy was assigned the less important post of Immigrant Absorption. The Liberal's most important cabinet position was Finance, held by its leader, Ehrlich. The Liberals persuaded Begin to keep three cabinet posts open for the DMC, should Begin's stalled negotiations with Yadin succeed in the near future.

Negotiations with the DMC

Prior to the election, Yadin promised his supporters he would not join any government that would not accept DMC's principles and its reform proposals. When Begin was able to form a government without the DMC, Yadin was left with the choice of making limited gains by joining the government or remaining true to the party's principles and accepting an opposition role.

Two issues in the protracted negotiations proved especially troublesome: the question of the West Bank and electoral reform. The DMC sought to base West Bank settlements on restrictive security grounds rather than Begin's ideological approach to Greater Israel and maintain a flexible position on territorial concessions. Yadin's formula was: "The people of Israel have a historic right to the Land of Israel and to the areas of Israel which have security importance."(27) The Likud was willing to modify its formula only by the insertion of a single word: "The people of Israel have an eternal (historic) right to the Land of Israel that is unchallengeable." Strenuous efforts to reach a compromise failed.

A similar impasse resulted from the negotiations on electoral reform, a high priority for the DMC. It wanted direct elections by districts

27. Torgovnik (Arian, 1977 Election), p. 91.

rather than the present single national constituency. During the negotiations DMC modified its original demand for creation of 20 electoral districts, reducing it to 16 and keeping some Knesset seats under the existing system. Begin agreed to 15 districts. The NRP, fearful that a radical change in the PR system would lead to its demise, proposed there be six districts. Begin then suggested a compromise on ten districts. Finally Begin gave the religious parties a veto in future legislation on the number of voting districts, which did not bode well for the DMC's commitment to meaningful electoral reform.

Begin offered to free the DMC from coalition discipline in votes on electoral reform and religious questions, and to allow the DMC to abstain in votes concerning the West Bank. Anticipating that this arrangement would reduce DMC influence in important Knesset votes, Yadin rejected Begin's offer. By September the Likud-DMC negotiations were stalemated. Some DMC members were reluctant to rationalize away their party's principles and join the Likud government simply for patronage gains. But veteran politicians like the DMC's Tamir and Amit were most reluctant to sacrifice their ambitions for cabinet posts. In the end Tamir and his supporters convinced Yadin that wielding even moderate influence inside government circles was preferable to having DMC shut out altogether. In October only a few days before the portfolios reserved for the DMC were to be given to other parties, the DMC council voted to approve the party's participation in a Likud government.

Yadin was appointed Deputy Prime Minister, and he would take over as Prime Minister when Begin was absent. He was empowered to coordinate social welfare ministries and control their budgetary allocations. Begin promised to support a shift in the electoral system to regional representation, but without disturbing the relative strength of the religious parties. Tamir took over the Justice ministry, while Amit was assigned Transport. Another DMC leader (Katz) became Minister of Labor. Yadin justified the DMC's decision by a perceived national emergency, presumed to arise from a threatened confrontation with the United States over the peace process. Rubinstein's Shinui faction deplored the DMC's decision to settle for less than half a loaf, and refused to be considered for one of DMC's four cabinet posts. He and some of his supporters boycotted the Knesset session that approved the new DMC ministers. In this early period the basis was laid for the DMC's later disintegration.

In coalition formation Begin initially formed a narrow coalition comprised of three parties, making substantive policy concessions to the religious parties as well as patronage pay-offs (three important cabinet posts). At the same time he strengthened his parliamentary support for Likud's nationalistic policies, which he accorded the highest priority. In the negotiations with the DMC, Begin had to make patronage pay-offs (four cabinet posts), but only marginal and ambiguously phrased policy concessions, which ultimately proved meaningless. At the end of the four-month process Begin had succeeded in enlarging his parliamentary base of support from 63 to 78 seats. But this substantial majority was subsequently subject to erosion, as Begin adopted innovative foreign policies, especially the peace treaty with Egypt.

III
The 1981 Election

(1)   The State of the Parties

The single most important policy innovation of the first Likud government (1977-81) was the signing of a bilateral peace treaty with Egypt in March 1979, after a 30-year period of intermittent warfare between Israel and the Arab states. The dramatic visit of Egypt´s President Anwar Sadat to Jerusalem in November 1977, initiated a period of intense diplomatic activity, which led to the Camp David accords between Israel and Egypt in September 1978, made under the aegis of U.S. President Jimmy Carter.

The Camp David agreement was divided into two parts.(1) The first part provided a complicated framework for negotiating a transitional autonomous regime in the West Bank and Gaza, pending a final settlement of their ultimate status. The second part proposed guidelines for the gradual return of the Sinai to Egyptian sovereignty. This involved abandonment of three Israeli air bases and withdrawal of Jewish settlements there, which provoked strong criticism from Likud hardliners.

1. See the author's *The Camp David Peace Process* (Grantham, N.H.: Tompson & Rutter, 1981)., pp. 30-33.

Negotiation of the Israeli-Egyptian treaty required a second intervention by President Carter to bring it to successful completion. The Israeli and Egyptian conceptions of Palestinian autonomy were sharply at variance, and despite U.S. intercessions, a compromise between the two positions proved impossible during the autonomy negotiations.

In domestic policy the most grievous problem was the Likud government's unsuccessful efforts to check the raging inflation, which by 1981 had risen to over 130 percent a year. Three different Finance Ministers--Ehrlich(Liberal), Hurvitz(La'am) and finally in 1981, Aridor(Herut), were successively appointed in a fruitless search for an effective economic policy.

The purpose of this section is to review briefly certain developments in the leading parties under the Begin regime. In several cases these were in large part responses to the policies of the Likud government.

Likud Defections

Begin's decision to agree to the evacuation of Sinai settlements and support an autonomous regime for the West Bank and Gaza had disruptive repercussions in the Likud bloc. In the Knesset vote on Camp David, Begin arranged that Likud MKs be exempt from coalition discipline. In this way Likud hardliners could vote against the agreement without automatically being excluded from the government.(2) Only 12 of 21 Herut MKs voted for the Camp David accords, the other nine either voting against them or abstaining.

Two Likud MKs--Guela Cohen and Moshe Shamir, later left the party and organized a new, ultranationalist party called *Tehiya* (Renewal). Cohen bitterly attacked the "turn-coat" Herut MKs, who approved the Camp David accords. In 1980 while the Palestinian autonomy talks were under way, she

2. "Likud in Power: Divided We Stand," David Pollock (in Freedman, op. cit.) pp. 32-33.

sponsored a bill providing for formal annexation of East Jerusalem, where Israel had exercised *de facto* control since 1967. In the Knesset vote Cohen's bill was supported by a solid majority. Cohen's second attempt to embarrass the Begin government by introducing a bill for annexation of the Golan Heights failed. The new rightist Tehiya soon attracted substantial support from followers of Greater Israel and Gush Emunim, and in 1981 entered a party list in the parliamentary elections.

The Likud government was seriously weakened by the resignations of two key cabinet ministers-- Foreign Minister Dayan and Defense Minister Weizman. Although Dayan had played a prominent role in the Camp David negotiations and the peace treaty with Egypt, Interior Minister Burg was placed in charge of the Israeli team for autonomy talks. Dayan became increasingly critical of the Government's "dilatory tactics" in these talks. In October 1979 he resigned his cabinet post. He was succeeded by the Herut hardliner, Yitzhak Shamir, who had been serving as Speaker of the Knesset. In the 1981 election Dayan organized a new centrist party.

As a leading member of the Likud cabinet, Weizman had repeatedly clashed with his acerbic colleague, Sharon. In 1978 prior to the Camp David conference, Weizman denounced Sharon's scheme to construct what he called "dummy settlements" in the Sinai, and threatened to resign, if their construction was not halted.(3) He also became critical of the slow pace of the autonomy talks and the Government's aggressive settlement policy on the West Bank. In May 1980, after a proposed cut in defense expenditures, Weizman resigned. Begin accepted with alacrity. In November 1980, Weizman voted against the Government on a close no-confidence motion, and the Herut's central committee summarily expelled him from the party.

3. Ibid., p. 36.

Factionalism in the Liberal Party

After the Likud victory in 1977, Simcha Ehrlich appeared to be in a relatively strong position as Liberal party leader and holder of the key Finance Ministry. In addition he had long enjoyed close relations with Menachem Begin. But his dismal record as Finance Minister made him vulnerable to a leadership challenge by ambitious younger party leaders, led by Energy Minister Modai and Trade Minister Gideon Patt.

To a limited extent an ideological difference overlay the Liberals' internal power struggle: the hawkish Young Turks versus the more moderate senior leader, Ehrlich. This was particularly the case for Modai, who had abstained on the draft treaty with Egypt and was a strong advocate of extensive Jewish settlements on the West Bank.

In a secret party ballot in 1979, Ehrlich was supported by only four out of 14 Liberal MKs. Shortly he was shifted to the largely symbolic post of Deputy Prime Minister. In political parlance he had been "kicked upstairs." In 1980 Modai became the new Liberal party leader.

Meanwhile Ehrlich bided his time. His Young Turk opposition was not a cohesive faction. With Begin's tacit support, he began to mend fences, and in 1981 managed to regain his party's leadership. It was clear, however, that more rounds in this factional strife were forthcoming.

Fissures in the DMC

Even as early as the coalition negotiations with the Likud in 1977, the DMC had revealed serious internal divisions. In 1978 shortly before the Camp David conference, the Shinui faction, led by Professor Rubinstein and supported by six other DMC MKs, suddenly shifted to the opposition. Rubinstein charged that under Prime Minister Begin the peace talks were stalled. As vocal members of the Knesset opposition, the small Shinui faction continued to criticize the Likud's policy of expanding West Bank settlements and spoke out vigorously for accelerating the peace process.

Subsequently two other DMC members defected and formed one-man Knesset factions. By the middle of 1979, the DMC's Knesset representation was reduced to six out of the original 15 members. In November Yadin was obliged to share his deputy prime ministership with Ehrlich, after the latter's resignation as Finance Minister.

In mid-1980 the DMC representation was again cut in half, when three more members defected and organized a small faction called *Ahvah* (Brotherhood). A few weeks later, the DMC's Justice Minister, Shmuel Tamir, resigned, pointing to the absurdity of having as many DMC cabinet ministers as members in the Knesset. To many observers the DMC's chances of surviving a second parliamentary election appeared slight.

Labor's Rehabilatory Effort

Stunned by the loss of the 1977 election, Labor party leaders encountered considerable difficulty in assuming the unaccustomed role of leader of the parliamentary opposition. Initially they seemed preoccupied with the search for scapegoats for the party's poor showing. Recrimination was the order of the day. Peres said that it was more the effect of the DMC campaign than Likud's appeal that explained Labor's setback. At the same time he acknowledged that it was the party's "own conduct" that "caused our ruin"(4), including the scandals associated with the Rabin government. In his memoirs Rabin blamed Peres for his downfall.

Early in 1978 after the initial Israeli-Egyptian talks bogged down, Peres attempted to capitalize on diminished public confidence in Begin's government. He sharply attacked the Prime Minister for Israel's share of the blame in creating an impasse. Some Labor doves supported the burgeon-

4. *The Jerusalem Post, International Edition,* September 12, 1977.

ing Peace Now Movement, which held a series of
successful mass rallies. Begin was incensed by
Peres' private talks with President Sadat in Aus-
tria, and the cabinet attempted to prevent opposition leaders from conducting such exchanges in the
future. Begin's statements in the Knesset became
increasingly vitriolic. When some Labor MKs questioned Begin's physical and psychological fitness
to rule, Begin's physician issued a statement
flatly denying Labor's charges, which Begin himself called "slanderous."(5)

Although the Labor party supported the Likud
government in both the Camp David and peace treaty
votes, Labor spokesmen voiced strong reservations
about both. They strongly criticized Begin's
decision to evacuate Sinai bases, but at the same
time attacked his restrictive version of Palestinian autonomy. Labor appeared to be the major
beneficiary of the Dayan-Weizman resignations and
also the announcement that Israel's inflation rate
had risen to the highest in the world, passing
Argentina. In October 1980 a public opinion poll
predicted that Labor would win an unprecedented
absolute majority of Knesset seats in the next
election.

New Directions for the NRP

The new leadership of the NRP that emerged in
the 1977 election sought to redefine the party's
traditional role in Israeli politics. Previously
NRP members in Labor coalitions had been mostly
preoccupied with protecting their religious constituency's parochial interests. The younger
party leaders like Education Minister Hammer,
urged his party to formulate positions on a wider
range of public policies and take a more active
role in coalition policy-making. At the same time
they favored opening up party membership to religiously traditional but non-orthodox elements,

5. "The Labor Party in Opposition," Myron J. Aronoff (in Freedman,
op. cit.) p. 88.

substantially expand its membership and thus become a serious competitor for control of the government. Contacts were established with an
organization of European Christian Democratic
parties, which the NRP could use as a model for a
reconstructed party. Within the party the more
conservative Burg faction was concerned that the
party's core of orthodox Jewish supporters would
be alienated by a large influx of non-orthodox
members and the NRP substantially weakened.(6)

No sooner had the NRP begun to adopt a new
format, than it was confronted with the prospect
of revolt by its extremist right wing. After
Young Guard members took important Government
posts in 1977, they moderated some of their earlier militant positions. In 1978 they accepted
Begin's Camp David policies, for which they supplied welcome votes. This shift greatly antag-
onized NRP hardliners, who continued to maintain
close relations with Gush Emunim circles. In an
attempt to avert a large-scale defection of NRP
extremists to the new Tehiya party and Likud, the
NRP leaders conducted a purge of the principal
party doves from the party list in the pending
Knesset election. Their earlier ambitious plans
for party reconstruction were indefinitely
shelved.

(2) The Campaign

A particularly striking feature of the 1981
election campaign was Prime Minister Begin's demonstrated ability to hold almost continuous center
stage to the discomfiture of his opponents, determine single-handedly the content of the major
campaign dialogue and within a few months radically improve his party's originally bleak electoral
prospects. For two years the Begin cabinet had
been riven by internal disputes and considerably

6. "Religious Parties and Politics in the Begin Era," Daniel J.
Elazar (Freedman, op.cit.) p. 109.

weakened by Dayan's and Weizman's departure. By
the end of 1980 the critically important Palestinian autonomy talks with Egypt appeared hopelessly
deadlocked, taking the gloss off Begin's earlier
triumph of making peace with Egypt, which was
widely considered his Government's major achieve-
ment. With Israel's annual inflation rate running
over 130 percent the Government's domestic performance came under severe criticism. The moment of
truth came November 19, 1980, when the Begin Government narrowly survived a Knesset vote of confidence on its economic policies by a 57-54 vote.
The Government had in effect lost its parliamentary majority.

The following January the Government's position
was further weakened by Finance Minister Yigael
Hurvitz's resignation due to the cabinet's decision to meet the wage demands of 60,000 teachers.
Hurvitz indicated he would form an independent
party to contest the next election. The die was
cast in February when the Knesset at the Likud's
initiative set June 30 as the election date.

In contrast to 1977 the Histadrut elections in
1981 were held nearly three months prior to the
Knesset election. Of the 1.5 million eligible
voters, only 57 percent voted. The Labor alignment won 63 percent of the vote, an increase of
nearly eight percent over its 1977 vote, while the
Likud vote at 27 percent was only slightly below
that of 1977. To some observers the Alignment's
loss of more than 200,000 votes (in absolute numbers) compared to 1977, made the outcome of the
pending Knesset election highly uncertain.

Early public opinion polls indicated that Labor
would form the next government by a margin of 58
seats over the Likud's 20. In April Labor still
held a lead of 46 seats compared to 35 for Likud.
In early May when the crisis in Lebanon was acute,
there occurred a dramatic shift with the two major
parties tied, each with 41 seats. In early June
Likud moved into the lead over Labor 45-42.(7)
Even taking into account a rapidly fluctuating

7. These findings were reported in a series of polls taken by the
Jerusalem Post; other polls showed a similar shift in voter preference.

undecided vote over this period, it was clear that Begin had moved from an initial position of almost certain defeat to a very close race with Labor, which the actual results subsequently confirmed. What factors explain this significant turn-around in voter preferences? Four considerations require comment here: Begin's exceptionally aggressive campaigning style; his shrewd manipulation of a series of foreign policy crises to his Party's advantage; the popular tax reductions put into effect by the new Finance Minister, Yoram Aridor; and Labor's generally ineffectual campaign performance under Shimon Peres' leadership.

Begin, the Feisty Campaigner

In contrast to 1977, Begin assumed an active role in the whole Likud campaign effort. As incumbent Prime Minister he was presented with opportunities for policy initiatives with a potential electoral pay-off. In June, for example, Begin arranged a summit meeting with President Anwar Sadat, a timely reminder to the Israeli voter of his Camp David achievements. Other even more important foreign policy moves will be considered below. At election rallies held in different parts of the country he was often rapturously received by huge crowds acclaiming him "King Begin." He invariably responded with blistering attacks on his opponents which were warmly received, especially in audiences in which Oriental Jews predominated. There could be little doubt that his charismatic mass appeal made him the center of the electoral campaign.

In a well-publicized imbrolgio with Chancellor Helmut Schmidt of West Germany, Begin showed how he could utilize a foreign target for domestic political advantage. In April Schmidt held discussions in Saudi Arabia on possible future German arms sales. Returning to Bonn Schmidt articulated the Germans' "moral duty" to support Palestinian Arab claims to the right of self-determination in the occupied territories. In the Palestinian conflict, Schmidt said, "one cannot simply assign all morality to one side and shrug away the other side."(8) Israel lodged an official protest with the West German Government. Begin launched an all-out attack on Schmidt, who, he claimed, was not aware "of the obligation toward the Jewish people of which Germany destroyed one third." Begin also employed the device of the calculated insult by a disparaging reference to Schmidt's war-time service in the Nazi Army, charging he had remained loyal to Hitler until the end. Though Begin's intemperate remarks caused an international furor, they were seen in Israel as boosting his electoral prospects.

Crises in Foreign Policy

In the critical phase of the electoral campaign there occurred two important foreign policy developments--first, the prolonged Syrian missile crisis in Lebanon beginning at the end of April and then Israel's bombing in June of the Iraqi nuclear reactor. Both riveted world attention on Israel and Prime Minister Begin. Begin's simultaneous holding of the Defense Ministry intensified his involvement in these developments. Internally these crises deflected public attention from the Government's serious domestic problems and enabled Begin to appear as staunch defender of the national interest. Whether the Government's involvement was partially motivated by electoral considerations became a campaign issue.

The background to the crisis in Lebanon was complicated. Since 1970 Lebanon had become the principal base of the Palestine Liberation Organization, and Israel subsequently acquired a strong interest in restricting hostile actions by Palestinian guerrillas across its northern border. In 1976 Syria intervened in the bitter civil war between the Lebanese Christians on the one hand

8. *The New York Times*, May 8, 1981.

and Lebanese Muslims and Palestinians on the other. The ostensible objective of the Syrian peacekeeping force was to establish a more even balance between the two opposing groups in face of an apparently imminent Christian defeat. The Israelis feared Syrian ascendancy in Lebanon would be adverse to their security interests.

In 1976 a "tacit understanding" with Syria over Lebanon was reportedly made by the Rabin Government under the aegis of U.S. Secretary of State Henry Kissinger. Only belatedly did its provisions become publicly known. In Rabin's version Israel accepted the Syrian entry into Lebanon, provided Syria would not cross a designated "Red Line" into southern Lebanon and that Syria would not use its air force against ground targets or deploy ground-to-air missiles in Lebanon.(9)

As the result of the Israeli invasion of southern Lebanon in March 1978, a buffer zone was set up at the border, divided between an area patrolled by United Nations forces and a Christian zone controlled by a renegade Lebanese Army officer, Major Saad Haddad, who in fact acted as an Israeli proxy. Later Israel began to send secret shipments of weapons and supplies to Christian Maronite forces in north Lebanon.

A new situtation arose early in 1981 when Phalangist Maronite militiamen under Beshir Gemayel attempted to break out of their autonomous enclave north of Beirut. Gemayel was quoted as defining the Phalangist goal as a "war of liberation" against the Syrians and Palestinian guerrillas. In Syrian eyes a successful Phalangist advance supported by a regular supply of Israeli arms would undermine the crucially important Syrian strategic position in the Bekka Valley. As fighting escalated between the Syrians and Christians the possibility of a decisive Syrian victory reactivated Israeli fears of a future Syrian takeover in Lebanon.

In late April a sequence of incidents led to a

9. Interview with Yitzhak Rabin, *The Jerusalem Post, International Edition*, May 24, 1981.

dangerous confrontation between Israel and Syria.
For the first time Syria used attack helicopters
against Phalangist positions. Israel promptly
dispatched American-made Phantom jets to shoot
down two Syrian helicopters as a demonstration
warning. Syria's response was to move Soviet SAM-
6 anti-aircraft missiles into Lebanon. Israel
then warned Syria that if its missiles were not
removed, the Israeli Air Force would take unilateral action to eliminate them. Syria defied the
Israelis and moved in more anti-aircraft missiles
and additional troops. The prospect of a full-
scale war between Israel and Syria now loomed as a
major threat to regional stability.

Under pressure from Washington Israel was induced to approve the mediatory mission of President Reagan's special envoy, Philip Habib, and
defer for the time being its projected air strike
against the Syrian missiles. But Prime Minister
Begin made it clear that Israel was unwilling to
grant the Habib mission an indefinite period of
time to produce results satisfactory to Israel.
In case of diplomatic failure the Israelis were
poised to take the military option, whatever the
consequences. Habib then began an unrewarding
round of talks with the principals in the crisis
with the important addition of Saudi Arabia, considered an influential voice in Damascus.

The crisis in Lebanon had an immediate impact
on the election campaign in Israel with Begin's
opposition claiming that he sought to make political capital out of the situation. A series of
raucous debates was held in the Knesset with a
spill-over effect at election rallies. The essential Government argument was that the introduction
of Syrian missiles jeopardized Israel's free use
of air space in Lebanon to make frequent aerial
surveillance flights and preemptive air strikes
against Palestinian bases, when deemed necessary.
To these pragmatic considerations Begin incongru-
ously added an emotionally charged issue in his
insistence that Israel would never tolerate "geno-
cidal acts" against the Lebanese Christians by
their foreign foes.

The opposition focused its attention on Begin's
startling admission that Israeli aircraft had been
prepared to strike against Syrian missiles three
different times on April 30, the day after they
were first introduced into Lebanon. Weather conditions had prevented actual launching of the
strikes. Begin was scathingly criticized for
publicly revealing the conditions under which the
Air Force would act.(10) His critics also argued
the Government had allowed itself to be pushed
into an unwelcome confrontation with Syria by
over-zealous Lebanese Christians in order to attain the latter's goal of driving out the Syrians.
The limited effectiveness of these attacks on
public opinion was seen in the Likud's dramatical-
ly improved position in opinion polls published in
May after the eruption of the Lebanese crisis.

On June 8 Israel launched a secret air attack
on Iraq's French-installed nuclear reactor which
caused world-wide repercussions. The negative
fallout to the Government was considerable. In
the U.S. the Reagan Administration condemned the
attack and temporarily suspended delivery of four
F-16s to Israel. At the United Nations the U.S.
representative, Jeane Kirkpatrick, collaborated
with the Iraqi delegate in sponsoring a Security
Council resolution "strongly condemning" the Israeli action, but stopping short of imposing sanc-
tions. Egyptian President Sadat, who held summit
talks with Prime Minister Begin three days before
the raid, expressed his "astonishment" at the
Israeli action. Israel's increased tensions with
the Arab world were expected to have a depressant
effect on the Habib mission and complicate the
ultimate resolution of the Arab-Israeli conflict.

The Iraqi raid injected a highly controversial
new issue into an already embittered campaign. In
a television appearance Chaim Herzog, head of the
Labor campaign, charged that electoral considerations contributed to the timing of the raid. In
the Knesset Labor called for the removal of "the
helm of state from Likud control" because of the

10. Ibid., May 17, 1981.

Government's irresponsible tendencies. The Likud in turn accused Labor of lacking "minimal patriotism, loyalty and responsibility to the basic safety of the nation."(11)

Begin and Opposition leader Peres became embroiled in an acrimonious dispute over the raid. On May 10 in a "personal top secret" letter to Begin, Peres urged him not to launch the Iraqi operation on that date. After the raid Peres publicly explained that his opposition to the May 10 date was due to its coincidence with the French national election. If Mitterand were elected President, there was hope in Peres' opinion that he might reverse the French policy of nuclear assistance to Iraq. Begin insisted that Peres had not only disagreed with the May 10 timing but had been opposed to the raid "on principle." Begin released the text of Peres' "secret" letter to the Knesset Foreign Affairs and Defense Committee to substantiate his contention. To some observers Begin's intent was to insinuate gross deficiencies in Peres' patriotism. Another Labor spokesman (Gur) charged that Begin in fact knew that the Iraqi reactor would not be activated in July and hence the raid was "premature."(12)

In opinion polling on the Iraqi raid, little support was registered for Labor's sharp attacks. Nearly 83 percent of those polled believed the Iraqi raid was justified, and more than 75 percent thought Labor's criticism of it, unjustified.

The Factor of Aridor's Tax Package

When Yoram Aridor succeeded Hurvitz as Finance Minister in January he introduced a radically new tax policy. Aridor's predecessors had unsuccessfully attempted to check rapidly rising prices by the device of curbing private expenditures. Aridor pursued the opposite course of encouraging a much higher level of consumer spending by a sweep-

11. *The Jerusalem Post*, June 10, 1981.

12. Ibid., June 11, 1981.

ing program of tax cuts. His method was to introduce a sequential round of tax cuts over a period
of several months. His first innovation was a ten
percent tax reduction on small and medium cars,
color television sets and most home electrical
appliances. Within two months an estimated
100,000 television sets, 5,000 cars and 20,000
electrical appliances were sold.(13) Extra
freight aircraft were required to bring in addi-
additional luxury goods from the U.S. and Western
Europe.

Aridor next introduced a special savings scheme
which was indexed to the cost-of-living, followed
by a substantial loan plan for young couples buying government housing. In March Aridor doubled
the number of wage-earners in the bottom quarter
of the tax bracket and halved the number in the
top 60 percent, which was expected to increase
consumer disposable income by 20 percent. Inheri-
tance taxes were to be abolished, as well as the
property tax on built-up real estate. The round
of tax cuts announced in April included air-condi-
tioners, motorcycles and motorbikes. Aridor con-
tended that lower prices in durable goods would
sufficiently stimulate sales, so Government reve-
nues overall would not be adversely affected. In
June it was reported that Aridor's total package
of tax cuts and loans amounted to one-tenth of the
current Gross National Product, an estimated 26
billion in Israeli shekels.(14)

Labor applied the derogatory label of "election
bribery" to Aridor's policies. It was predicted
that after the election there would be a severe
backlash to the Government's "spending spree" and
a very rapid acceleration in the inflation rate.
For itself Labor espoused an economic program of
extreme austerity with tight controls on consumer
spending which it claimed would bring down
inflation to a 30 percent rate. To Labor's dismay
the public response to Aridor's policies appeared
overwhelmingly favorable.

13. *The Economist* (London), March 7, 1981.

14. *The Jerusalem Post*, June 5, 1981.

The Labor Party's Campaign Effort

With the approach of the 1981 election, the Labor party was confronted with yet another divisive contest between Peres and Rabin for party leadership, beginning with Rabin's announcement of his candidacy in October 1980. Peres held certain advantages over his long-time rival. After the 1977 debacle Peres traveled widely throughout Israel in a painstaking effort to rebuild the party organization starting at the grass-roots level. He also led successive parliamentary assaults on major policies of the Likud government. In organizing his campaign Rabin relied heavily on his supporters in one of the powerful kibbutz federations *(Hameuchad).*

Peres made careful preparations for the party conference in December 1980, that would decide the leadership question. Leading European socialists, including Francois Mitterand, attended the conference, as well as a high-level Egyptian delegation. Peres delivered the main address. In the 1977 contest Rabin had defeated Peres by a narrow margin. This time, as a reflection of his organizational skill, Peres won a majority of 70 percent, gaining 2,123 votes out of a total of 3,028.(15) Rabin's less than gracious concessionary speech indicated that Labor's long succession crisis had not been resolved. Early in 1981 Rabin's supporters fought hard to secure representation proportionate to their strength in the party's new central committee.

Peres' choice of Labor's shadow cabinet (i.e. the major ministerial appointments, were Labor to form the next government) aroused fresh controversy. Rabin, who aspired to be the next Defense Minister, was left off the list entirely. For shadow Finance Minister, Peres' first choice was Yaacov Levinson, head of Histadrut's Bank Hapoalim. When Peres refused to guarantee Levinson certain discretionary powers in economic matters, Levinson declined the appointment. Peres then turned to Professor Chaim Ben-Shahar, president of

15. Aronoff in Freedmen, op. cit., p. 93.

Tel Aviv University, who was a trained economist
but had little experience in party affairs. As a
compensatory move, Peres then announced that Ben-
Shahar would head an economic "troika" and share
decision-making with two other party appointees.
Oddly, Ben-Shahar was not given a safe seat on the
Labor party list. Peres was strongly criticized
for having passed over Rabin in naming his shadow
cabinet, and on the eve of the election he dumped
his original choice for shadow Defense Minister,
Chaim Bar-Lev, and replaced him with Rabin.
Peres' critics claimed the excessive time given to
discussions over the shadow cabinet had adversely
affected Labor's campaign effort.

Peres' "secret" meetings in March with King
Hassan II of Morocco and a brother of Jordan's
King Hussein were seen as a major gaffe, and laid
him open to the charge he was trying to usurp the
Government's foreign policy role. Against the
Likud opposition Peres seemed unable to capitalize
on the Government's weaknesses, especially the
soaring inflation rate and the recurrent pattern
of cabinet disputes. Foreign policy issues, where
the Government had a clear advantage, dominated
the campaign from late April to the end of June,
allowing Prime Minister Begin to command media
attention almost on a daily basis. In the case of
the Lebanese crisis and the furor over the Iraqi
raid, Peres had the difficult task of criticizing
the Government on national security matters without bringing his own loyalty into question. Finally Peres' stolid campaign style was no match
for Begin's flamboyance.

Despite its inept and divided leadership the
Labor party could still mobilize substantial
campaign resources.(16) These included the
Histadrut infrastructure and its affiliated
kibbutzim, moshavim and industries. In the Hebrew
daily press Labor advertised more extensively than
the Likud, roughly 77,000 inches to 47,000. As
one of the two largest Knesset parties it had a

16. *The Elections in Israel--1981*, Asher Arian. (Tel Aviv:
Ramot Publishing Co., 1983), p.7.

substantial block of free television time. The fleet of cars and special workers available to Labor on Election Day were greater than any other party's. But these impressive assets were insufficient to match Begin's skillful manipulation of the rising tide of Israeli nationalism.

The Passing of the DMC and the New Party Entrants

The withdrawal of Professor Yadin's DMC from the political scene in February introduced an important element of uncertainty in the outcome of the 1981 election. The immediately relevant question was who would inherit the some 200,000 votes cast for the DMC in the 1977 election. Would Labor recoup most of the substantial number of votes it lost to DMC, or would the DMC vote be unevenly dispersed among several parties? Their distribution would have a major impact on the 1981 electoral results.

In his valedictory speech Yadin blamed the DMC's failure both on the Shinui faction's splintering tactics and the naivete of his own political leadership.(17) Yadin's task had been formidable: to keep his heterogeneous coalition in line, and fit a presumably reformist party into a rightwing Likud government. His political leverage was weak, when it became clear that DMC's adherence to Begin's government was not essential to its survival. In retrospect the DMC's main function appeared to be its serving as the electoral instrument in 1977 through which disaffected Labor voters registered an effective protest and turned the Labor party out of office.

In 1981 there were three untried contenders who were expected to play a significant role in the outcome. These were the rightwing Tehiya, Moshe Dayan's centrist party and an important new ethnic party.

17. *Jerusalem Post, International Edition*, February 22, 1981. Yadin claimed major credit for the favorable Knesset vote on the peace treaty with Egypt.

The Tehiya party. The chief organizational
feature of the new Tehiya was its admixture of
supporters: both religious zealots and secular
nationalists. Considered mostly a single issue
party, Tehiya was strongly committed to the retention of the occupied territories and their incor-
poration in an enlarged Eretz Israel. It
attracted support both from orthodox Jews in Gush
Emunim and the more secular Land of Israel movement. In the campaign the party was headed by
Professor Yuval Ne'eman, a leading nuclear physi-
cist, who proved an effective spokesman.

The Tehiya accused Prime Minister Begin of
"selling out" in the Sinai, and argued that dismantling the Israeli settlements there would set a
precedent for other occupied territories. To
members of Tehiya, Begin also appeared "soft" on
the Palestinian issue, since the Camp David accords made reference to the "legitimate rights" of
the Palestinians. The introduction of an autonomous regime would inevitably lead, Tehiya claimed,
to the establishment of a Palestinian state, hostile to Israel. Tehiya advocated a much reduced
Palestinian population on the West Bank, pointedly
noting the Palestinians had 22 Arab states to
choose as emigration sites.(18)

Dayan's party vehicle. Considered by many observers to be one of Israel's half-dozen most
outstanding leaders since 1948, Moshe Dayan remained an enigmatic political figure, the quintes-
sential maverick. Due to Prime Minister Eshkol's
equivocal policy in the buildup to the 1967 war,
Dayan had played a decisive role in the formation
of a national unity government. His record as
Defense Minister in the Meir government in the Yom
Kippur War led to a crisis in Labor party leadership and a temporary eclipse in his political
fortunes. In party-dominated Israel, Dayan's
acceptance of the Foreign Ministry in a Likud
government was highly controversial. His partici-

18. Further to the right Rabbi Kahane, head of the Kach list,
assailed the Tehiya for being "soft" on the Palestinian issue.
He advocated expulsion of Arabs from both the occupied territories and Israel.

pation in the Camp David conference in 1978, which
he later described in a detailed account called
Breakthrough, was critically important. By many
of his colleagues Dayan was viewed as arrogant,
disinclined to suffer fools gladly. Few observers
were surprised when he announced the formation of
a new centrist party, called *Telem* (State Renewal
Movement), in April 1981. Speculation was widespread that if his party won a half-dozen Knesset
seats, it would play a crucial role in the formation of the next government.

Dayan encountered considerable difficulty in
putting together a coherent campaign organization.
Characteristic of the Telem campaign was the
strenuous effort to enlist the talent of former
Finance Minister Hurvitz, who attempted to form
his own independent party. Late in the campaign
he finally joined the Telem's slate.

Dayan's most important policy position was his
proposal for a unilateral Israeli imposition of an
autonomous regime in the occupied territories.
His call for withdrawal of Israel's military government on the West Bank while the occupation
continued, provoked considerable controversy. In
future negotiations with Jordan, Dayan insisted
that Israel retain vital strategic areas on the
West Bank.

Although early polls showed that Telem would
win a sizable number of Knesset seats, Dayan's
campaign never acquired significant momentum. In
the end his party was primarily dependent on a
remnant of the Rafi party. In a curious way
Dayan's final political stand paralleled that of
his mentor, Ben-Gurion.

A new ethnic entry. The formation of *Tami*
(Movement for Israeli Tradition) in June under the
leadership of Religious Affairs Minister, Aharon
Abuhatzeira, as a splinter off the National Religious Party(NRP) marked the reemergence of the
ethnic factor as a significant force in Israeli
politics. Except in the first two Knessets ethnically based parties had failed to pass the one
percent "threshold." The NRP was particularly
subject to internal tensions due to the discrepan-

cy between its large numbers of Oriental Jewish voters and the domination of its leadership by East European Orthodox Jews. Announcement of the new party was made after Abuhatzeira's acquittal on bribery charges in distributing Ministry funds.

To his supporters Abuhatzeira's subjection to a sensational public trial appeared racially motivated. The precipitating factor in his break with the NRP was a bitter show-down fight over the relatively few number of North African Jews in preferred positions at the top of the NRP electoral list. Abuhatzeira, himself a Moroccan, conceived Tami chiefly as a vehicle for North African Orientals to challenge "Ashkenazi discrimination."

The campaign coffers of Tami were enriched by donations from its chief patron, the Swiss-Jewish millionaire, Nessim Gaon, supplemented by contributions from wealthy Oriental Jews in the United States. In campaign statements the NRP decried the "buying" of political power by foreign millionaires.

Abuhatzeira attempted to broaden Tami's narrow base beyond its nucleus of NRP secessionists by naming Aharon Uzan, former Agriculture Minister in the Labor government and also of Moroccan extraction, chief campaign coordinator and No. 2 man on the Party list. Tami's primary focus appeared limited to winning new power positions for Oriental Jews in future governments and espousing a hard-line nationalist position on the territorial question. Its entry into the campaign made it likely the NRP would incur some loss in Knesset seats.

The Nomination Process

Few changes were made in the 1977 innovations in the nomination process (see Chapter II).

In the Likud there had occurred a significant change in power relations between the Herut and its two major partners, the Liberals and the La'am party. Prior to 1977 Herut had been dependent on the votes of its two smaller allies to become an effective competitor of the dominant Labor party. After the Likud victory in 1977, the Liberals and La´am became dependent on Herut for their political survival. In view of this reversal, Herut leaders proposed that the Likud parties abandon their separate autonomous nominating processes. Parliamentary candidates would be elected by a general Likud convention in which there would be no separate party quotas. The Liberal party rejected this proposal.

In 1981 the Herut´s central committee, the party organ designated to select Knesset candidates, was enlarged from 640 members in 1977, to 900 in 1981.(19) On the first vote taken, Prime Minister Begin was elected unanimously to the first position on the Herut list. On the second vote the committee screened 74 persons, who were contesting the 35 places on the Herut list. In successive voting rounds the ranking of the candidates was determined.

The Herut made a determined effort to increase representation of Oriental Jews. Though the party leadership is essentially Ashkenazi, Oriental Jews now comprised the majority of party members and were an increasingly important segment of the Herut electorate. In 1981 about a fourth of Herut´s electoral list were Oriental Jews. These were more than token nominations, and included mayors of several important development towns.

There was a considerable rivalry for the No. 2 slot between three party leaders: Housing Minister Levy, a Moroccan Jew; Agriculture Minister Ariel Sharon, closely identified with the Government´s activist settlement program in the occupied territories; and Ya´acov Meridor, Begin´s long-time friend and associate from Irgun days. In the central committee vote, Levy won the No. 2 position, Meridor took third and Sharon won the sixth slot.

In the Labor party two new informal party

19. "Nominations in Israel: the Politics of Institutionalization," Giora Goldberg and Steven A. Hoffman, in Arian 1981 Election volume, p. 62.

groupings had since 1977 become increasingly influential in party circles.(20) The first of
these was the *Beit Berl* group, comprised of a
number of liberal intellectuals, holding moderate-
ly dovish views. Among its members was Ya´acov
Levinson, a leading party economic expert. The
second group called *Yahdav* was by contrast more
trade union and Histadrut-oriented, more hawkish
in outlook, more Oriental in composition. Yahdav
was led by two Tel Aviv party officials, Eliahu
Speiser, secretary of the district party, and Dov
Ben-Meir, secretary of the powerful Histadrut
workers´ council. Both groups had helped Peres
defeat Rabin for party leadership.

The major innovation in Labor´s nominating
procedure was the more important role assigned the
party´s district branches. First an extremely
small elite group called the "arranging committee"
was set up, comprised of Peres, Rabin, Bar-Lev,
the party´s secretary-general, and one representative each from the Yahdav and Beit Berl groups.
Its main job was to hear various delegations of
party activists and determine the shares of the
list assigned to the regional party branches--
which branches would receive safe seats and how
many. But key decisions on the ranking of individual candidates were taken by an informal committee, which included besides Peres six members:
the leaders of two kibbutz movements, the moshav
movement and in the three major cities--Tel Aviv,
Haifa and Jerusalem. The dominant members of this
group were Speiser, leader of the Yahdav group
representing the Tel Aviv district, and Uzi Baram,
secretary of the Jerusalem district and member of
the Beit Berl group. Rabin failed to get the 30
percent of the party list, which he claimed for
representatives of his faction. Rabin himself was
assigned the No. 4 slot on the Labor list.

The selection of the No. 2 position next to
Peres proved contentious. The two rivals were
Abba Eban, a long-time party leader, and Shoshana
Arbelli-Almozlina, who had recently been voted the

20. Aronoff in Freedman, op. cit., pp. 81-82.

most popular of veteran Labor MKs. Mrs. Arbelli had several advantages: she was an Oriental Jew, a group in short supply in the top Labor leadership; she was expected to attract the women's vote; and her hawkish views balanced the dovish stance of Peres' shadow cabinet. Abba Eban, who warned he might defect if he failed to get the No. 2 position, was persuaded to make way for Mrs. Arbelli and accept third place. The leader of the Mapam party, Victor Shemtov, was listed as No. 5. In the end Labor named 18 Orientals--less than a third of its list (but more than Likud), and for the first time included an Arab candidate in what appeared to be a safe slot.

The Eruption of Campaign Violence

As the campaign drew to a close, there was mounting public concern over the unprecedented level of politically motivated violence. Rhetorical excess is a norm in Israeli politics, but the 1981 campaign produced an ugly combativeness. Its chief features were the systematic disruption of Labor Party rallies and a visible pattern of threats and assaults against Labor's supporters.(21) The perpetrators were rowdy gangs of pro-Likud toughs, including some younger Orientals. At Shimon Peres' rallies they frequently jeered him off the platform, pelted him with eggs and tomatoes and drowned out his speeches with chants of "Begin, Begin, king of Israel." In some cases windows in Labor Party headquarters were smashed and Labor leaflets burned. Persons wearing Labor campaign buttons were subject to harassment, store windows with Labor posters smashed and cars with Labor bumper stickers had tires stolen and windshields cracked. By the last week of the campaign the police had arrested 157 persons charged with committing 171 electoral offenses.(22)

21. *New York Times*, June 25, 1981.

22. *Jerusalem Post, International Edition*, June 28, 1981.

The Likud leadership denied responsiblity for
these incidents and deplored recourse to violence.

Peres launched a sharp counter-attack against
this sudden eruption of violence, viewing it as a
"battle over Israel's democratic soul."(23) Israel's slippage into "autocratic rule with an
idolized leader and Khomeini-like statements"
would never be permitted, he said. Another Labor
candidate(Hillel) charged Begin's supporters with
"trying, via accepted and familiar methods...to
pave the way toward fascism in public life."
Likud spokesmen claimed Labor was exaggerating the
significance of violent incidents to its own
political advantage.

Several different interpretations were advanced
in the media to explain the marked increase in
violence. Some observers pointed to the fall-out
effect of Begin's frequent use of inflammatory
statements, especially allusions to the "disloyal-
ty and treason" of critics of his Government's
policy in Lebanon and the Iraqi raid. Others
stressed the limited exposure of large numbers of
Oriental Jewish immigrants to democratic methods,
having grown up in authoritarian Arab regimes and
unaccustomed to self-imposed restraints necessary
in parliamentary systems. Acts of campaign violence were seen by some critics as a logical
extension of the increasingly harsh methods which
the Israeli Army used to suppress Palestinian
nationalist demonstrations and the related militant tactics of the Gush Emunim in provocatively
locating its settlements in major centers of Palestinian population. An extreme example of this
latter interpretation was that of Jacobo Timerman,
the exiled Argentine publisher then living in
Israel, who expressed fears that Israel was "going
to totalitarianism and fanaticism." In Timerman's
view Gush Emunim was a "fascist movement," whose
tactics closely paralleled the clandestine armies
and terrorists he had observed in Argentina.

23. *New York Times*, June 25, 1981. The cited statements on political violence were published in the *Times*.

The Begin-Peres TV Debate

The televised debate between Begin and Peres was the last major event of the campaign and provided the electorate with a summation of major issues.(24) A single journalist-interlocutor was employed to question the two men. Somewhat unexpectedly Peres was aggressively on the offensive, Begin mostly on the defensive. Peres made a scathing attack on Begin's economic performance: an inflation rate of 1210 percent over four years, a significant slow-down in development and immigration and a reckless pre-election give-away to the voters under the Government's program of tax cuts. Begin took credit for a 13.5 percent increase in real wages over four years and boasted that Israel had no unemployment problem. Peres argued that the campaign had been the most violent in Israeli history and that he himself had been victimized by character assassination. In rebuttal Begin said his political opponents had blackened his name for years and referred back to the pre-1948 era when Labor's predecessor, Mapai, betrayed members of Begin's Irgun to the British authorities.

On the issue of closing the ethnically based "social gap" Peres promised Labor would work for a more just society, sponsoring such measures as cheaper housing mortgages for young couples. Begin pointed to the 135,000 "housing solutions" already made by Likud for persons "left without civilized housing" by the last Labor Government. His Government had also instituted free secondary education and rehabilitated 70 neighborhoods, Begin said.

On foreign policy matters Peres accused Begin of making "high flying speeches" on the Syrian missile crisis and criticized the Iraqi raid for putting President Sadat in an "impossible situation" and jeopardizing the peace process. Begin replied that in his pre-raid talks with Sadat, he would not of course reveal an Israeli military

24. *Jerusalem Post, International Edition,* June 28, 1981.

secret. On the controversial autonomy issue Peres
said Israel would be left "without peace," if
autonomy talks failed. Begin blamed Sadat for the
stalled autonomy talks. Peres charged that Begin
still planned to annex "Judea and Samaria"(the
West Bank), which would make Israel a binational
state diluting its Jewish character. Begin was
scornful regarding Labor's "Jordanian option"
which would return the Samarian mountains to Jordan's Hussein, who would in turn give them to PLO
leader Arafat, and after that "Katyushas will be
fired at Tel Aviv."

(3)   Election Results

The 1981 election, the closest in Israel's
history, ended in a virtual deadheat for the two
leading parties, 48 seats for Likud and 47 for
Labor. Clearly the party system was in a prolonged transitional phase, begun when the "earth-
quake" election of 1977 ended Labor Party
dominance but with its ultimate outcome still in
doubt. The poor showing and even extinction of
some of the left-liberal and radical parties indicated a further rightward shift in the elctorate's
preferences. Even more important the closeness of
the outcome confirmed what the fractious electoral
campaign had alrady made clear--that Israel was
riven by serious ethnic, social and policy con-
flicts. Concern was voiced that a succession of
close elections like that of 1981 would ultimately
undermine Israel's democratic system and increase
public yearning for the alternative of a militar-
istic, strong-man regime. Yet the passing of
polling day without serious violence, the continued high voter turnout rate of 78.5 percent--
only slightly below 1977, and the workings of the
customary process of inter-party accommodation in
forming a new coalition government partially mitigated some of these fears.
Thirty-one Party lists were entered in the 1981

election. Twenty-one of these failed to pass the
one percent threshold. The remaining ten parties
shared in the distribution of seats compared to 13
parties in 1977. In 1981 there were 2,490,140
eligible voters, an increase of approximately
254,000 over 1977. Slightly over a half-million
voters did not cast ballots in 1981, proportion-
ately somewhat more than in 1977. (See Table II.)

A special feature of Israeli elections is that
the vote of the IDF is separately counted and
reported. As expected the IDF vote favored rightwing nationalistic parties. The Likud received
45.8 percent compared to Labor's 34.1 percent.
Four smaller rightist parties received an additional 12.5 percent. Both the Likud and the
rightist Tehiya parties received significantly
higher proportions of the soldier vote than their
respective shares of the civilian vote.

In the distribution of Knesset seats under the

TABLE II

1981 Election Results

Party	Votes	%	Knesset Seats
Likud	718,941	37.1	48
Labor Alignment	708,536	36.6	47
National Religious Party	95,232	4.9	6
Agudat Yisrael	73,312	3.7	4
Democratic Front	64,918	3.4	4
Tehiya	44,700	2.3	3
Tami	44,466	2.3	3
Telem	30,600	1.6	2
Shinui	29,837	1.5	2
CRM	27,921	1.4	1
Others	99,903	5.2	0
Total	1,937,366	100.0	120

PR system 113 seats were allocated in the first round. In accordance with the complicated Bader-Ofer system the Likud gained two of the seven "surplus" seats, the Labor Alignment one. Four of the smaller parties--Tehiya, Telem, Tami and Shinui, each received one additional seat. The use of this method provided Likud with its narrow margin of victory.

The Predominance of the Two Major Parties

For the first time the Likud and Labor parties won nearly 80 percent of Knesset seats and approximately 75 percent of the popular vote, which were unprecedentedly high percentages. In 1981 the smaller parties won 25 seats compared to 45 seats in the 1977 election.

Most analysts concluded that Israel was moving in the direction of a two-party system. Certainly the predominance of the two leading parties reflected the highly personalized nature of the 1981 campaign. For many voters their choice was essentially between two men--Begin and Peres. Under what was called the "mutual aversion" principle(25) a significant number of the electorate voted against an opposition candidate rather than positively *for* a party of its choice. Many Labor voters were seen as primarily concerned with avoiding another four years of a Begin government, while conversely some Begin voters, recalling the Labor scandals of 1977, were determined to block Labor's return to power. The leaders of nearly all the smaller parties attributed the precipitous drop in their support to the marked trend toward voter polarization between Likud and Labor.

In its own right the Labor alignment enjoyed a substantial recovery in its electoral fortunes, increasing its Knesset representation over 1977 by 50 percent with the addition of 15 new seats and also its percentage of the popular vote by 11.9 percent. Two important factors in Labor's im-

25. *New York Times*, July 2, 1981.

proved position were the return of the bulk of
Labor's defectors to Yadin's DMC in 1977 (DMC had
won 15 seats then) and a significant shift in the
Arab vote away from the Communist-dominated Democratic Front in favor of the Alignment's list (see
below). In addition there were two developments
in the last days of the campaign which were considered favorable to Labor. One was Peres' assertive stance in his televised debate with Begin--a
Gallup poll indicated that 54 percent of the
viewers judged Peres the winner. The second was
Peres' sharp attacks on Likud-inspired campaign
violence which redounded to Peres' benefit.

For its part the Likud not only managed to
sustain its 1977 record but somewhat improved its
position, winning an additional five seats and
increasing its popular vote by nearly four points.
Besides Begin's virtuoso campaign performance the
chief contributory factors were the breaking of
foreign policy developments during the campaign in
the Likud's favor, the Likud's advantage in
corralling the larger percentage of Oriental votes
(see below) and evident public approval of
Aridor's program of expanded Goovernment subsidies
and tax cuts. Doubts remained, however, that the
long-term electoral prospects of either Labor or
Likud were in fact as promising as the 1981
results suggested.

The Weakened Position of the Smaller Parties

Almost across the board the remaining eight
parties that won Knesset seats either incurred
serious losses or failed to sustain their original
promise(26). None of the three important new
parties won sizable voter support. Moshe Dayan's
Telem party got only two seats. Two former cabinet ministers on Telem's list (Hurvitz and Katz)
failed to win seats. Since most of Telem's support came from Labor rightwingers, Telem apparently lost votes by not renouncing in advance future
participation in a Likud-led government.

26. *Jerusalem Post, International Edition*, July 5, 1981.

Instead of the predicted five or six seats the
ultranationalist Tehiya captured only three seats
with party leader Ne´eman and the well-known MK,
Geula Cohen, heading the list. After Rabin was
appointed to Labor´s shadow cabinet, some Tehiya
supporters shifted to Likud, which Ne´eman claimed
was caused by last-minute fears of a Labor victory. Not surprisingly Tehiya made an impressive
showing among Jewish settlers in the occupied
territories. It captured 23 percent of their
vote, compared with only 2.3 percent in the country as a whole.

Abuhatzeira´s Tami party won only three seats
instead of the anticipated four or five. Even so
Tami was the first ethnic party to make a fairly
impressive electoral showing since the 1950s. Its
vote came almost exclusively from Jews of North
African background, who comprise the largest Oriental group in Israel. While Tami appeared to be
essentially an ethnic party, Abuhatzeira could
also exploit his background as member of a prominent rabbinical family in Morocco and make religious appeals to his constituency. Certain of
Tami´s organizational weaknesses--such as Abuhat-
zeira´s continued legal entanglements, cast a
shadow over the party´s future prospects.

Of the established smaller parties the NRP
suffered the most severe setback. It lost half
its Knesset seats, being reduced to six mandates,
and its popular vote dropped from 11.6 percent in
1977 to a low point of 4.9 percent. Clearly the
NRP paid a heavy price for having failed to placate Abuhatzeira´s faction by increasing Oriental
representation on the party list. NRP losses to
Tami were especially heavy in development towns in
south Israel, where many North African Jews live.
But the NRP also suffered substantial losses to
both the Likud and Tehiya parties.

Parties on the left-liberal end of the political spectrum were dealt a crippling blow. Two of
these failed to pass the one percent threshold--
the Independent Liberal Party, once a frequent
coalition partner in Labor-led governments, and
Shelli led by a mixed collection of maverick left-

wing politicians. Amnon Rubinstein's Shinui, once
aligned with Yadin's DMC in Begin's cabinet and
holder of seven Knesset seats, was reduced to two.
Rubinstein claimed that "droves" of Shinui supporters fled to the ranks of Labor in order to
prevent Begin's return to power.(27)

The Citizens' Rights Movement(CRM), led by
Shulamit Alloni, barely qualified for a single
seat. Shortly after the election Mrs. Alloni
merged her party with the Alignment, giving Labor
48 seats and exact parity with the Likud. Finally
the Communist-dominated Democratic Front for Peace
and Equality lost one of its five Knesset seats,
and its percentage of the popular vote dropped
from 4.6 to 3.4 percent. The immediate political
consequence of the shrinkage in Knesset representation for the left-liberal parties was that it
seriously reduced the number of coalition allies
Labor could attract in forming a new government.

Of the smaller parties it was only the ultraorthodox Agudat that sustained its parliamentary
position of four seats as in 1977 and held approximately the same percentage of the popular
vote, slightly under four percent. Preoccupied
with religious questions, the compact body of
Agudat supporters is less susceptible to shifting
currents of electoral politics. Its one-time
partner in electoral alliances, Poali Agudat, did,
however, lose its single Knesset seat.

The Increased Importance of the Ethnic Factor

During the 1981 campaign there was considerable
evidence of a resurgence of ethnic politics. In
addition to the emergence of Abuhatzeira's Tami
Party there were four ethnic protest lists: *Ihud,*
led by two MK's (Elgrabli and Marciano);
One Israel, headed by another MK (Yitzhaki; *Am-
cha,* organized by a former Black Panther (Tayar);
and the *Ohalim* movement. Their appearance reflected the increasing impatience of Oriental Jews

27. Ibid.

with their second class status. Particularly
offensive to members of these groups is the widespread practice of "tokenism"--that is, including
representative Orientals on lists of Ashkenazi-led
parties without changing the pattern of Ashkenazi
domination. These several protest parties failed,
however, to generate a significantly large vote.
Only the Tami Party won Knesset representation.
Together the five parties polled slightly over
50,000 votes and under three percent of the popular vote.

Clearly Oriental Jews had opted for the mainstream of Israeli politics, but they divided their
support for the two major parties very unevenly.
In its social base the Likud was becoming increasingly an Oriental party, and the Labor alignment,
a predominantly Ashkenzai party. In 1981 about
two-thirds of Likud voters were of Oriental background, while about 70 percent of Alignment voters
were of European descent. A striking feature of
the 1981 campaign was the close correlation between ethnic tensions and eruption of campaign
violence--especially in the street clashes between
Likud and Labor supporters, when racial slurs were
frequently lodged against Peres. For the first
time since 1948 communal tensions themselves became a major campaign issue.

Gonen has traced out the spatial diffusion of
the increased Likud vote among the Oriental population since the 1965 election.(28) The first
Likud breakthrough occurred in the old inner urban
neighborhoods of the three large cities (Tel Aviv,
Jerusalem and Haifa). Support for the Likud
spread first to immigrant housing developments on
the outskirts of the old cities, becoming marked
by the 1973 election. In the 1969 election the
Likud vote surpassed that of Labor in the immigrant towns that, beginning in the 1950s, developed near the old cities. In 1977 the vote in new
development towns with their predominantly Oriental populations swung decisively to the Likud.
The cumulative effect of this diffusion process

28. "A Geographical Analysis of the Election in Jewish Urban
Communities" in Caspi, Diskin, and Gutmann, op. cit., pp. 78-80.

was reflected in the Likud's winning more than half the Oriental vote in 1981.

What factors explained the increased preference of Oriental voters for the Likud? First the Labor party had the disadvantage of having been the Establishment party during the heaviest years of Oriental immigration in the 1950s. Many of these persons were "dumped" in development towns in the desert without adequate attention to their special needs. Some Labor Government bureaucrats held patronizing attitudes toward the new migrants, which were deeply resented. Many of them filled the lower ranks of semi-skilled labor with insufficient income to care for their characteristically large families. Even as the out-party, Labor is hobbled with this legacy. Some observers assert that for many Orientals, their vote for Likud is a "spite" vote against Labor.

Secondly the Likud's hawkish stance and opposition to Israeli withdrawal from the occupied territories dovetailed with the views of many Oriental Jews.

Finally there was the special factor of the rapport between Menachem Begin and his Oriental constituency, despite Begin's Polish background. In 1981 they constituted his most enthusiastic audiences at campaign rallies and were responsive to his uninhibited rhetoric and feisty defiance of Israel's enemies. Like the Orientals, Begin was for years an "outsider," scorned by the Establishment. Begin was a political pariah; they were social pariahs. Even more importantly Begin was careful in his public functions to respect the rituals of Jewish religious tradition, which was warmly appreciated by many Oriental Jews. Even as head of a government short on redressing Oriental grievances, Begin could still draw on an almost unlimited reservoir of their good will.

Changes in the Arab Vote

Under the Likud government there occurred an
intensification in the process of "Palestinianization" of the half-million Israeli Arabs.--i.e.
their increased identification with the plight of
Palestinian Arabs in the occupied territories.(29)
Previous Labor governments were at least formally
committed to the "full integration of the minori-
ties," and Histadrut spokesmen had referred to
"partnership" between Israeli Arabs and Jews.
Statements by Begin government ministers, however,
often placed Israeli Arabs in the same category as
Arabs living under Israeli military occupation.
Increasingly Israeli Arabs expressed a strong
sense of solidarity with Arabs in the West Bank
and Gaza.

In the spring of 1980 the political situation
on the West Bank became exceptionally tense. Extensive new land expropriations by the Begin government, punishment curfews and outbreaks of
violence resulted in the deportation of the mayors
of Hebron and Halhul in May, and bomb attacks on
the mayors of Nablus, Ramallah and El-Bireh in
early June. The Begin government failed to un-
cover the perpetrators of these incidents. In
Israel proper the Rakah (Communist) party took the
lead in calling for a conference of Israeli Arabs
to organize a political struggle against the Government's "iron fist policy" in the occupied territories. At a preparatory meeting held in
September, it was decided to hold a full Congress
in Nazareth in December, when the Arabs would seek
official recognition as a "national minority." On
December 1, Prime Minister Begin banned the Nazareth Congress, and Justice Minister Moshe Nissin
stated that the Congress represented an attempt to
"promote separation" and establish a separate Arab
entity in Israel.

Earlier a group of Arab university students,
chiefly at Hebrew University in Jerusalem, had

29. "Israel's Arab Minority in the Begin Era," Ian Lustick in
Freedman, op. cit., p. 136.

organized a group called the Progressive National Movement(PNM). The PNM set itself apart from Rakah, rejecting alliances with "progressive forces" among the Jewish majority (Rakah had a mixed membership). The PNM and Rakah proceeded to wage a bitter struggle for the allegiance of Arab student organizations on Israeli campuses.

These developments directly affected the Arab vote in the 1981 election.(30) A significant number of Arabs reasoned that if they cast their vote for the Rakah's electoral front--DPFE, they might insure the reelection of the Begin government, hostile to Arab interests. It would be preferable, they reasoned, to vote for the Labor alignment, despite Labor's past record of neglect of the Arab minority. The proportion of Arabs voting for the Labor party or its affiliated list increased from 27 percent in 1977 to 36 percent in 1981. Rakah's share of the Arab vote decreased sharply from 71,000 (49 percent) in 1977 to 59,000 (36 percent) in 1981. The Labor-affiliated list, however, did not qualify for a Knesset seat. Due mainly to the election boycott of the PNM and other Arab radicals, the Arab turnout rate dropped to a new low of about 69 percent. Whether the considerable decline in the Arab Communist vote indicated a more pragmatic Arab approach in Israeli politics remained problematic.

(4) Summary

Like previous elections the 1981 election provided important evidence of significant changes in the party system. Some of its major features were as follows:

Shift toward a competitive party system. In 1977 when the long domination of the Labor party was terminated, some observers were uncertain as

30. Ibid., p. 144.

120

to whether Labor would reassert its dominance in
1981. Although Labor's electoral showing markedly
improved over 1977, it only achieved near parity
with the Likud. Israel appeared to have moved
toward a new phase of intense competition between
the two leading parties. In most Israeli elec-
tions--even in the period just before the 1977
election, the electorate expected that despite
possible variations in Labor's voter support, it
would form the next government. In 1981 neither
of the two parties was certain of the outcome.
The turnaround in the opinion polls between their
prediction of a Labor victory in April and a
reversal in Likud's favor in June, indicated a
marked volatility in the electorate.

A surprising feature of the 1981 results was
the coalescence of three-quarters of the electorate behind the two major parties, compared to 58
percent in 1977. Whether this result portended an
irreversible trend toward a two-party system was
uncertain. Some observers argued the unexpected
increase in the combined Likud-Labor vote merely
reflected the intense desire of some center-left
voters to avoid a second Likud government, and
conversely the determination of some rightist
voters to prevent Labor's return to power.

The enhanced importance of the ethnic vote.
Most observers agreed that more than in any previous election, the 1981 contest demonstrated the
mounting importance of the ethnic factor in determining voter allegiances. The evidence included
the following points: 1)emergence of Abuhatzeira's Tami party, organized to mobilize a protest vote against Ashkenazi domination among North
African and other Oriental voters; 2)the attempt
of both major parties to woo Oriental voters, now
the largest component in the electorate, by assigning Orientals to prominent places--including
the No. 2 spot in both Likud and Labor, on their
respective electoral lists; 3)heavy reliance of
the Likud, despite its Ashkenazi leadership, on
votes of Oriental Jews, combined with the increasingly Ashkenazi composition of the Labor electorate; and 4)Labor's attempt to make the violent

outbreak of racial tensions a major campaign issue.

Factional splintering and the floating vote. The continued importance of the floating vote was partly a reflection of fissiparous tendencies in several parties. The splintering off of Tami from the NRP was a major factor in the NRP's loss of half its Knesset seats. In addition the support of NRP MKs for Begin's Camp David agreements prompted some of NRP's rightwing supporters to defect to the Tehiya. In the Likud bloc the Herut party lost votes to Tehiya, led by Herut defectors, but Herut offset this loss by attracting new rightwing voters. Dayan's centrist party relied heavily on defectors from Labor's rightwing, but this loss of Labor's was partly compensated by its winning votes from such dovish parties as the Shinui, CRM and Shelli.

The centrality of the personality factor. Not since David Ben-Gurion had a party leader held such a commanding position in a parliamentary election as Menachem Begin in 1981. Despite factional splinterings in his Likud bloc, Begin mobilized an impressive parliamentary majority for the first peace treaty made with an Arab state, for which Begin won the Nobel Peace Prize. In the 1981 campaign Begin's tactics insured the primacy of foreign policy developments, which were politically favorable to the Likud, and enabled him to shunt his party's dismal record in domestic economic policy to the background. He was the widely admired champion of Israeli interests against Iraq and Syria. He was the chief beneficiary of heightened racial tensions, expressed at Likud's mass rallies, where Begin was invariably the object of mass adulation. Although he headed the government for nearly four years, Begin was still widely viewed as an anti-Establishment figure with strong appeal to working-class Oriental Jews.

By contrast Labor's Peres appeared as a routine leader presiding over a party torn by inner conflict, reflected in the prolonged contest for party leadership with Rabin. Peres' prerogatives in party appointments were adversely affected by

the practical necessity of assigning some party
posts to the Rabin faction. The weakness of his
position was underscored by his last-minute re-
placement of Bar-Lev with Rabin for shadow Defense
Minister.

*Increased professionalism in party campaign
tactics.* In the 1977 campaign Ezer Weizman won
plaudits for his professionally smooth operation
of the Likud effort. In 1981 both leading parties
attempted to professionalize their campaigns by
relying heavily on public opinion surveys and
hiring American campaign advisers, David Garth for
the Likud and David Sawyer for Labor. In the end
the imported advisers were only marginally effective. Foreign policy developments, so favorable
to the Likud, diminished Garth's role. Peres'
failure to provide effective overall direction of
the campaign minimized the importance of Sawyer's
contribution.

Disproportionate use of broadcast time. The
two leading parties continued to enjoy enormous
advantages over the smaller parties in access to
free broadcast time on radio and television, since
parties with Knesset representation are allocated
additional free time in accordance with their
relative parliamentary strength. In the 1981
election the Likud had 250 minutes of television
time in contrast to the small CRM's 16 minutes.(31)

(5) Coalition Formation

In 1981 as in previous elections neither Likud
nor Labor won a parliamentary majority, thereby
necessitating a multiparty coalition cabinet. The
closeness of the vote between the two major parties provided an extraordinary opportunity for the
religious parties to play a crucial role in forming a new government. In the case of NRP, declin-

---

31. "The Professionalization Trends in Israeli Election Propaganda 1973-81," D. Caspi and C. H. Eyal in Arian 1981 Election
Volume, p. 236.

ing voter support at the polls was followed paradoxically by enhanced power in shaping the new government.

At the outset Likud enjoyed an advantage over Labor in prospective number of coalition allies. Of the eight smaller parties in the new Knesset Begin could expect at least an initially receptive hearing from five parties with a total of 18 seats, whereas Labor was reasonably sure of support from two parties (Shinui and CRM), holding three seats. Begin moved quickly to consolidate his advantage, and Labor's outside chance of leading a new government--by including Telem, Agudat and tacit support from Rakah--never materialized.

Begin began coalition talks immediately after the June 30 polling day and claimed by the end of the first week to have set the baselines for his new government. On July 15 after two days of consultations, President Yitzhak Navon took the anticipated course by formally asking Prime Minister Begin to try to form a new government. Two factors slowed the negotiating process. One was the effort of the religious parties to exploit fully their pivotal Knesset position and extract the maximum concessions to advance their interests. The second was a sudden flare-up in the Lebanese crisis, precipitated by Israel's bombing of Beirut starting July 17. At several points in five weeks the negotiations were at an impasse. Finally on August 4 after a last-minute flurry of intensive bargaining, Begin's new government was in place.

Patronage and Policy Issues

Begin was confronted with a two-fold task in building his coalition government. First within the Likud bloc itself distribution of ministerial posts as between the larger Herut Party and the Liberal Party, for whom Deputy Prime Minister Simcha Ehrlich was principal spokesman, had to be arranged. Secondly Begin had to assign specific portfolios to his potential coalition allies outside the Likud bloc and reach agreement with them on the terms of the Coalition Agreement. The latter task proved difficult and required most of Begin's attention for five weeks.

In dealing with the Liberals, Begin initially proposed the allocation of one cabinet post for every four Knesset seats which would have strongly favored Herut. Under pressure from the Liberals this formula was modified to a 1-3 ratio. In the end Herut gained eight cabinet posts to the Liberals' six in an 18-man cabinet. But in addition to the Prime Minister's office, Herut made a clean sweep of the "Big 3" ministries--Defense(Sharon), Foreign Affairs(Shamir) and Finance(Aridor). Shamir and Aridor were hold-overs in their posts. Sharon succeeded Begin at Defense.

Begin also had to intervene in an acrimonious dispute in the Liberal camp over the assignment of the Ministry of Trade portfolio, for which Gideon Patt and Yitzhak Modai were in strong competition. Begin opted in Patt's favor, and Modai was compensated by being named Minister Without Portfolio. The third and smallest Likud faction (La'am) was assigned one cabinet post.

In his contacts with the smaller parties, Begin's negotiations with Moshe Dayan and his Telem delegation came to naught. The long-standing disagreement between Begin and Dayan on Palestinian autonomy in the occupied territories persisted. Dayan had advocated a unilateral Israeli military withdrawal to accelerate the autonomy process. In a confrontational stituation Begin produced a copy of the text of the Camp David agreement, which he claimed proved that Israel was fully entitled to maintain its military government in the West Bank and Gaza. Begin was also subjected to heavy pressure from some NRP leaders not to appoint Dayan head of the autonomy negotiations. Begin himself favored the appointment of the NRP's leader, Yosef Burg.

Deputy Premier Ehrlich was assigned to put out feelers to the rightist Tehiya party regarding its possible support. But Begin's determination to proceed with full Israeli withdrawal from the

Sinai by April 1982 continued to meet strong opposition from Tehiya leaders. With Telem and
Tehiya virtually eliminated as coalition allies of
Likud, the need for completing successful negotiations with the religious parties became urgent.

Crucial negotiations ensued with three of the
smaller parties--the NRP, Agudat and Tami--which
together held 13 Knesset seats. Both patronage
and policy issues were at stake. As in 1977 the
Agudat under instructions from the Council of
Sages disavowed entry in the cabinet and acceptance of ministerial posts. The votes of its four
MKs would, however, help insure the Likud a parliamentary majority. In return the Agudat expected to have a decisive voice in formulating
provisions of the Coalition Agreement which dealt
with religious questions.

The Agudat's major demand, supported by the
NRP, was to amend the Law of Return, under which
every Jew has an automatic right to Israeli
citizenship. Under the proposed change only
conversions made in accordance with *halacha*
(Jewish religious law) would be recognized in
Israel. Conversions performed by Reform or
Conservative rabbis would be rendered invalid.
The proposed amendment raised once again the
highly sensitive question of "Who Is a Jew?" Both
inside Israel and in Jewish circles abroad,
especially in the United States where Reform and
Conservative adherents predominate, there were
angry denunciations of the Agudat proposal.

In the Likud bloc the Liberals declared they
were unalterably opposed to the Agudat's amendment. Begin stated that while the amendment was
personally acceptable to him, he could not compel
his Liberal cohorts to vote against their conscience. Strenuous efforts were made to find an
acceptable compromise. At one point it was proposed that in lieu of an actual amendment, the
rabbinical courts in Israel could be used to rule
on the acceptability of conversions performed
abroad.

A further complication arose when two influential Orthodox spokesmen--Rabbi Goren of the Chief

Rabbinate and the Rabbi of Gur, the co-chairman of
the Agudat's Council of Sages--jointly supported
an explicit amendment to the Law of Return recog-
nizing only *halacha* conversions. At the end of
July Begin introduced his own compromise formula
that once his Likud Government took office, he
would "work for" amending the Law of Return "at
the opportune time." The Agudat sought a less
equivocal assurance. The question was only finally resolved with adoption of the Coalition Agreement (see below).

When coalition negotiations began there was
considerable doubt that Begin would be able to
induce both the NRP and Abuhatzeira's Tami party
to enter his cabinet, so serious were the frictions between them. Abuhatzeira's last-minute
withdrawal from the NRP to form his own splinter
party before the election was viewed by NRP leaders as a main cause for their electoral setback in
June. Apparently only the NRP's keen interests in
patronage enabled its leaders to acquiesce in
Tami's joining the cabinet. For his part Abuhatzeira made entering the cabinet contingent on his
retaining the powerful Ministry of Religious Affairs, which he held in the first Begin government. As a "traditional" NRP ministry, the NRP
leaders wanted Religious Affairs returned to them.
Begin's problem was to work out some mutually
satisfactory distribution of portfolios between
the two rivals to insure the 61 votes he needed to
form a government.

Begin used several tactics to avoid an exces-
sively prolonged period of negotiations. As soon
as he was named by President Navon, Begin indicated that he would limit his efforts to a single
three-week period. If he failed, he would return
his mandate to the President, which he predicted
would lead to new elections within five or six
months. None of his future coalition partners was
eager to risk fresh elections and possible further
deterioration in their positions.

At a carefully staged press conference early in
the negotiations, Begin set certain limits on

patronage demands of the NRP and Tami parties.(32)
With only three Knesset seats Tami could expect
one minister. To Begin its demands for two ministers were "political bribery." The NRP with six
seats would get no more than two ministers. If
Tami and the NRP failed to resolve their dispute
over Religious Affairs and Tami opted out of the
coalition, Begin would return his mandate, and new
elections would shortly follow. Begin also made
clear that he would refuse to form a minority
government of 58 seats with only the NRP and
Agudat as partners. Finally he served notice on
the Agudat that he would not compel members of his
Likud bloc to vote in favor of amending the Law of
Return.

When the furor over Israel's bombing of Beirut
arose in late July, Begin tried without much success to use the crisis atmosphere it engendered to
accelerate the coalition negotiations. In a final
flurry of intensive bargaining before the expiry
of his self-imposed three-week deadline, Begin
somewhat modified his original strictures on allocation of ministries, and a new formula was devised for amending the Law of Return which the
religious parties accepted.

*The New Cabinet Line-up and the Coalition
Agreement*

The disparate elements in the prolonged negotiating process fell into place during the final
sequence of bargaining sessions prior to August 4.
First the dispute over patronage between the NRP
and Tami was settled. Tami's Abuhatzeira was
induced to relinquish the Ministry of Religious
Affairs, which was taken over by the NRP leader,
Dr. Burg. Burg was again awarded the Interior and
Police ministry and appointed to head the autonomy
negotiations with Egypt. Together these posts
constituted a formidable concentration of ministerial power. His rival in the NRP leadership,

32. *Jerusalem Post, International Edition,* July 19, 1981.

128

Zevulun Hammer, retained his post of Education Minister. Tami's Abuhatzeira was compensated for losing Religious Affairs by gaining both the Ministry of Labor and Social Welfare and the Immigration Absorption department. Tami's two other MKs were assigned deputy ministerial posts. For two small parties controlling only nine Knesset seats these were substantial patronage pay-offs.

Secondly a compromise in the controversial question of amending the Law of Return was reached, and incorporated as a critically important section in the Coalition Agreement. Resorting to qualified language Begin pledged to "make every possible effort" to secure Knesset passage for an Agudat-sponsored amendment on Orthodox conversions. Agudat leaders indicated that if Knesset passage were delayed beyond Passover in the spring of 1982, they would withdraw support from the Begin Government.

Unexpectedly Abuhatzeira's assignment to the Absorption Ministry with its considerable patronage caused a fracas inside Begin's Herut Party, which cast light on its internal rivalries. The previous holder of the Absorption post, Minister of Housing David Levy had reluctantly vacated it to make way for Abuhatzeira. As North African Jews Levy and Abuhatzeira compete for preferment in the same constituency. More importantly Levy was piqued because his major Herut rival as Begin's successor, Ariel Sharon, had been promoted from Agriculture Minister to the key post of Defense Minister. As an additional irritant Sharon had been instrumental in arranging Abuhatzeira's shift to the Absorption ministry. On the eve of Begin's first public announcement of his new government Levy suddenly decided not to remain in the cabinet as Minister of Housing to the dismay of his colleagues. After considerable behind-the-scenes maneuvering a new deputy premiership was created for Levy, which advanced him in the ministerial hierarchy. Levy was mollified and ended his single day hold-out.

Begin's most controversial cabinet appointment was Ariel Sharon as Defense Minister. Although

widely acclaimed a brilliant general, certain
facets of his long military career had in the past
been severely criticized. In the 1950s Sharon was
identified with the initiation of retaliatory
guerrilla warfare against the Palestinian *feda-
yeen*. His commando unit was involved in a highly
publicized raid on the Jordanian border town of
Qibya in October 1953, killing 69 persons, half of
them women and children. In the early 1970s as
military commander of the Gaza Strip, the pacifi-
cation campaign he waged against Palestinian terrorists was so unrestrained, that he was removed
from his command.

As Minister of Agriculture Sharon became one of
the most active supporters of a greatly expanded
program of Jewish settlements in the occupied
territories. In the cabinet he aroused the ire of
the Defense establishment with his strong public
statements in favor of cutting the military budget
as an anti-inflationary measure. When Ezer Weizman resigned as Defense Minister in the first
Likud Government, the prospect of Sharon's replacing him aroused so much criticism, Begin himself
took on the job. Begin's decision after the 1981
elections to appoint him to the Defense post, to
which Sharon had so long aspired, was apparently
partly prompted by fears of Sharon's defection, if
he were passed over again.

At the last minute his imminent appointment
came close to precipitating a break-down in the
coalition negotiations. A "dovish" NRP member of
the Knesset, Avraham Melamed, was so opposed to
Sharon's appointment, that he threatened to absent
himself from the Knesset vote of confidence on the
new government. Melamed argued that Sharon was
too strong a personality and in too important a
ministry to be effectively controlled by a government with a single-vote majority. Only when Melamed's party leader (Burg) threatened to resign as
Minister of Interior, did Melamed fall into line
and insure a favorable vote.

Begin's submission of the Coalition Agreement
to the Knesset revealed the full scope of the
concessions he felt impelled to make the religious

parties, especially Agudat. Thirty of its 83 provisions dealt with religious questions.(33) New restrictions were placed on certain activities during the Jewish Sabbath. Virtually all public transportation would be halted. The national airline, El Al, would be grounded on the Sabbath at an estimated cost of $50 million a year. The busy ports of Haifa, Ashdod and Eilat would be closed down on the Sabbath and Jewish holidays, adversely affecting their considerable traffic in tourist cruise ships. Government-owned companies like railways and oil-drilling organizations must in future cease work on the Sabbath. University dormitories occupied jointly by men and women would be abolished. A greatly expanded program of financial aid was initiated for students in *yeshivot* (religious schools).

In an important supplementary letter addressed to the Agudat parliamentary group, Defense Minister Sharon committed the new Government to a highly controversial policy of granting military exemptions to persons enrolling in Orthodox religious schools. In Israel where compulsory military service is regarded as essential to national survival, this latter concession provoked public criticism, even from some NRP members.

The clause in the Coalition Agreement (No.83) containing Begin's personal pledge on amending the Law of Return, was cited above. Somewhat anomalously Clause No. 42 of the Agreement stated that "the existing *status quo* on religious subjects will be preserved," despite the substantial changes which the Government had sanctioned. The Agudat party also shared in the distribution of patronage, being assured it would retain certain chairmanships of Knesset committees.

After bitter Knesset debate, Begin's new government was approved August 5 by a close vote of 61-58. In his opening statement Begin attempted to bolster his new governnment's legitimacy by pointing out that Likud won a plurality in ten of 17 polling districts, with the seven won by Labor

33. *The Jerusalem Post*, August 6, 1981.

being located in the less densely populated areas.
Labor's Shimon Peres in turn pointed out that the
Labor Party's 50 percent increase in its popular
vote in the 1981 election was the largest of any
party. Coupled with the votes of the CRM, which
had merged with Labor, it represented a larger
total than Likud's.

In his major speech Peres made caustic reference to coalition negotiations which had dealt
only with the budgets of the *yeshivot* and not the
defense budget.(34) He sarcastically inquired why
the NRP that had initially intended to have a
"spiritual stocktaking" after its loss of six
Knesset seats, had ended up "counting portfolios."
He scored the Tami Party for having caused the
departure of Morocco-born David Levy from the
cabinet by its takeover of the Absorption Ministry. As the day-long exchanges wound down, their
vitriolic content increased, as in Begin's reference to Peres--stated in English--"the gentleman
is a liar; the gentleman is a liar."(35)

Important policy statements by the new government were included in the Knesset debate. Surprisingly, Prime Minister Begin indicated Israel's
willingness to resume diplomatic relations with
the Soviet Union, provided Moscow would take the
initiative and also allow more Soviet Jews to
enter Israel. He defended Israel's recent bombing
of the Iraqi reactor and its military operations
in Lebanon as the "inherent natural right" of a
nation for its own self-defense, in accordance
with the United Nations Charter and the Locarno
Pact. Begin made clear that he did not believe
the recently concluded cease-fire in Lebanon restricted Israeli photoreconnaissance missions
there, and anyone interfering with such flights
would "bear the consequences." Fully aware of the
importance of relations with the United States,
Begin reported some easing of recent tensions with
Washington. He cited the President's reiteration

34. Ibid.

35. *New York Times*, August 6, 1981.

of American support for Israel and also Reagan's statement that Jewish settlements in the occupied territories were not illegal, a departure from the Carter Administration's position. Regarding a possible treaty witn the United States, Begin said it was "more proper for the big power to take the initiative." But with "aggressive totalitarianism on the march" Begin viewed a "joint stand for a common cause" with the U.S. as much needed.(36)

   Summary.   In both the 1977 and 1981 cases, Begin demonstrated considerable skill in difficult coalition negotiations.   Due to unresolvable policy differences with both Tehiya and Telem, Begin was, as in 1977, forced to opt for a narrow coalition, this time with three small parties, which together held the critical 13 seats needed for a parliamentary majority.   To induce the NRP and its splinter Tami to join his government, Begin made substantial patronage pay-offs to both. In the case of the small ultraorthodox Agudat, Begin felt obliged to make sweeping concessions on religious subjects.   With only four Knesset seats, the Agudat was identified with 36 percent of the items in the 1981 Coalition Agreement.   The Agudat was also rewarded with the chairmanship of the Knesset Finance Committee, which facilitated the channeling of increased government appropriations to its religious schools.   Despite the gains made by the religious parties, Begin, as in 1977, re-tained firm control over national security policies.
   Compared to 1977 the second Likud government appeared to be considerably more cohesive.   It had lost the DMC on its left flank, and its most hawkish members on the right had defected to form Tehiya.   Within the Likud bloc the relative power position of the Liberals had further declined. They no longer held the key cabinet post of Finance Minister and their position on Greater Israel had moved closer to that of the Herut.   The Knesset position of La'am was halved in the 1981

36. *The Jerusalem Post*, August 6, 1981.

election. But after Sharon's appointment as Defense Minister, speculation arose as to whether Prime Minister Begin could effectively restrain the actions of so formidable a political figure.

IV
The 1984 Election

(1)   Backdrop to the Election

The Invasion of Lebanon

The decision of the second Begin government to invade Lebanon in June, 1982, had momentous political consequences. Initially viewed as a bold Israeli attempt to tilt the Middle East balance of power decisively in its favor, the war in Lebanon ultimately proved highly destabilizing, both in its impact on Israel's external position and the durability of the Likud government. By 1983 the problem of the PLO threat in southern Lebanon which precipitated the war, had been replaced by a smouldering Lebanese Shiite rebellion against the prolonged presence of Israeli troops there. In September Prime Minister Begin resigned his leadership post, an action widely attributed to the high costs--both human and material, of the Lebanese war. His resignation was followed by the formation of a new government under Foreign Minister Shamir, which after seven months in office was compelled in March, 1984, to call new parliamentary elections.

The Lebanese war was Israel's first "optional"

war, in the sense that it was not preceded as in previous wars by a major military crisis, perceived as threatening the very foundations of the Israeli state. The attempted assassination of the Israeli ambassador to Great Britain in June, 1982, was used by the Government to justify the Israeli invasion in Lebanon and launch a war that had been long in preparation. The formulation and execution of basic war strategy was chiefly in the hands of Prime Minister Begin, Defense Minister Sharon and IDF Chief of Staff Rafael Eytan. Of the three Sharon played the decisive role, and in some quarters Israel's Lebanese enterprise was called "Sharon's war." The Israeli Cabinet was never fully informed regarding the full scope and precise objectives of the war. In certain military actions Sharon reportedly did not keep Begin informed.

At the outset the Government insisted that the war's limited objective was to establish a cordon sanitaire 25 miles inside southern Lebanon and eliminate the chronic threat of PLO artillery and missile firings into northern Israel. This would allow an early Israeli withdrawal. But shortly the IDF launched a massive assault on West Beirut, and Israel's broader range of objectives--both military and political, became evident. Its sweeping military objectives included the destruction of the entire PLO infrastructure that constituted a "state within a state" in Lebanon, elimination of an important center of international terrorism, outright expulsion of the PLO from its primary base in Lebanon, and withdrawal of the Syrian military from Lebanon. Its less obvious political objectives appeared to be the following: (1)using the Lebanese war as a diversion to shift world attention away from the Israeli attempt to consolidate its hold on the occupied territories; (2)manipulation of political developments in communally divided Lebanon to insure the primacy of Maronite Christians in a pro-Israel government; and (3)by demonstrating once again Israel's clear and overwhelming military superiority, inducing the Arab states to accept a negotiated peace settlement, favorable to Israel´s security interests.(1)

The initial widespread domestic support for the Lebanese invasion was seriously undermined by the Government´s complicity in the massacre of Palestinian civilians at the Sabra and Shatilla refugee camps by Lebanese Phalangists between September 16 and 18, 1982. Under pressure of parliamentary and public criticism the Begin government in October reluctantly appointed a three-member commission of inquiry, headed by the president of the Israeli Supreme Court, Justice Yitchak Kahan, whose function was to clarify Israel´s role in the massacres. Its findings, announced in February, 1983, were adverse to the Begin government and led to an important reshuffling of the Cabinet.

The Kahan Commission rejected the contention made by some members of the Government that Israel bore no responsibility for "deeds perpetrated outside of its borders by members of the Christian (Lebanese) community against the Palestinians."(2) The commission held that Israel did bear "indirect responsibility" which had a twofold character: (1)in granting the Lebanese Phalangists permission to enter the Palestinian camps, the Israeli command failed to give adequate consideration to the danger the Phalangists would in fact "commit massacres and pogroms;" and (2)that once high Israeli officials had been informed of the ongoing massacres, "no energetic and immediate actions were taken to restrain the Phalangists and put a stop to their actions."

In allocating the responsibility to key officials, the commission found variable degrees of involvement. Its findings regarding four officials--Prime Minister Begin, Defense Minister Sharon, Foreign Minister Shamir and Chief of Staff Eytan, were particularly important and had immedi-

1. "Israel and the Peace Process," Harold M. Waller, *Current History* 82 (1983) no. 480.

2. The full text of the report of the Kahan commission was published in the *New York Times* February 9, 1983, pp. 6-8.

ate repercussions.(3)   Prime Minister Begin was
found remiss in showing "absolutely no interest"
in Phalangist activities for a period of two days
after he heard about their entry into the camps.
It was argued that if Begin had manifested interest, Sharon and Eytan would have been more "alert"
to the need to take "appropriate measures." But
Begin's culpability was not considered sufficiently grave to warrant his resignation.

The case against Defense Minister Sharon was
regarded as more damaging, and the Kahan commission recommended either his resignation or dismissal. Sharon was accused of "blunders" tantamount
to "non-fulfillment of duty." He had failed, the
commission said, in not foreseeing the massacres
when he approved the Phalangist entry in the
camps, and in not issuing orders that would insure
control of their actions. Foreign Minister Shamir
was censured for not transmitting early information he had received regarding the massacres, but
the commission stopped short of calling for his
resignation. Chief of Staff Eytan was sharply
criticized for "dereliction of duty" in disregard-
ing the high probability the Phalangist militia
would take unrestrained action against the Palestinians. Since Eytan was scheduled to retire from
the IDF within two months, the commission decided
it would be impractical to call for his resignation. Among its other recommendations the commission called for the immediate dismissal of the
Director of Military Intelligence, General Yeho-
shua Saguy, for his "inattention, indifference and
negligence."

The release of the Kahan report precipitated an
anti-Government street demonstration of approximately one thousand persons in Jerusalem, organized by the reactivated Peace Now Movement,(4)
which led to violent clashes with militant Government supporters. A hand grenade exploded in the

3. Ibid., pp. 7 and 8.

4. Earlier the Peace Now Movement had mobilized public support
for negotiations leading to the Israeli-Egyptian Peace Treaty
in 1979.

large crowd outside the Prime Minister's office,
killing one of the demonstrators and wounding nine
other persons, including the son of Interior Minister Burg. The opposition Labor party called for
full implementation of the Kahan report, but deferred a decision on calling for immediate resignation of the Likud government.

After some delay the Cabinet voted 16-1 to
accept the Kahan report. The sole dissenting vote
was cast by Sharon, who insisted he would not
resign. The Cabinet was internally divided as to
Sharon's future governmental role. An influential
group of ministers--including Deputy Prime Minister Levy, Foreign Minister Shamir, Communications
Minister Zipori (all rivals of Sharon), and the
Liberal party leader, Deputy Prime Minister Ehrlich, attempted to block Sharon's retention. The
Tehiya party leader, Ne´eman, wanted Sharon to
continue to play an active policy-making role.
Prime Minister Begin engineered a compromise solu-
tion: Sharon would leave the Defense Ministry,
but remain in the Cabinet as Minister without
Portfolio. In addition he was assigned to two key
committees--a steering committee to carry on Israel's negotiations with Lebanon and an advisory
committee on defense matters. In this way the
Government adhered to the letter of the Kahan
report, while retaining Sharon as an influential
member of the Government. Moshe Arens, a key
figure in Israel's aeronautical industry and most
recently Ambassador to the United States, was
named the new Defense Minister. There was little
or no evidence that Sharon had been chastened by
his removal from the Defense Ministry, and within
six months he was a major competitor for the Begin
succession.(5)

In March the Begin government suffered another
setback when a member of the Labor party opposition, Chaim Herzog, a former general and Israeli

5. In a public speech at the time of his resignation Sharon depicted himself as a martyr to the cause of Israel's national
security. He claimed that the Reagan administration favored his
removal from office since he was regarded as an obstacle to the
creation of a Palestinian state. *New York Times*, February 13,
1983.

representative at the United Nations, was elected
President of Israel. Seven Begin supporters in
the Knesset defected to insure Herzog's election.

The May 17th Agreement

In the aftermath of the Sabra and Shatilla
incident the Government sought to reduce the
mounting domestic opposition to the war and consolidate its gains in Lebanon by negotiating a
withdrawal agreement with the Lebanese government.
Four months of difficult negotiations with the
Gemayel government, climaxed by the active intervention of U.S. Secretary of State George Shultz,
were required before a compromise agreement was
reached May 17, 1983.(6) It committed the Israeli government to withdrawal of its troops in
southern Lebanon in return for continuing security
arrangements, which included the following:
(1)establishment of a security zone in Lebanon,
running 20 to 37 miles north of Israel's northern
border; (2)provision for patrolling the zone by
eight Lebanese-Israeli teams and two Lebanese Army
brigades that would maintain direct communications
with IDF officers; and (3)restriction of Lebanese
military deployments in the south both in numbers
of troops and types of weapons. Once Israeli
troops were withdrawn, negotiations between the
two signatories for normalizing the movement of
goods and people across the Israeli-Lebanese fron-
tier were scheduled to begin within six months.
The Israeli government had to settle for an exchange of liaison officials with Lebanon rather
than establishment of full diplomatic relations.
Implementation of the Agreement rested on simultaneous withdrawal of Syrian and Palestinian forces from Lebanon. American efforts to induce
President Assad to order a Syrian withdrawal
proved unavailing.

6. The full text of the May seventeenth agreement between Israel
and Lebanon was published in the *New York Times* May 17, 1983,
pp. 4-5.

In Israel there was widespread dissatisfaction with the terms of the May 17th Agreement. Considering the nearly 500 Israelis killed and 2,700 wounded, many Israelis expected a more substantial and less conditional agreement. Ariel Sharon, the war's chief architect, argued that what Israel had won on the battlefield, had been lost at the negotiating table. He claimed that the arrangements for joint patrols and a territorial Lebanese brigade were insufficient to prevent the PLO's return to southern Lebanon. Opposition leader Shimon Peres criticized the accord as "too little and too formal." The previous informal arrangement in Lebanon, Peres said, had provided Israel with more security than the new agreement. Mapam's party organ said the Begin government had come "empty-handed out of an adventure" that it had described as the 'first war to yield political fruits'...the emperor is now revealed in all his nakedness."(7) A member of the Likud government, Energy Minister Modai said he would not have voted for the war at the outset if he had known "such limited gains would result."

The Cabinet voted 17-2 to accept the Agreement, with Sharon and Ne'eman casting dissenting votes. The Knesset subsequently approved it, 57-6, with 45 abstentions, mostly by Labor party MKs. Due to Syrian intransigence the highly touted Agreement remained a dead letter. Virtually Israel's only gain was that its strained relations with Washington improved, and the Reagan administration resumed arms shipments, which it had earlier suspended.

In September the IDF unilaterally redeployed its troops south of the Awali River, vacating both the environs of Beirut and the Shuf area, scene of armed clashes between Lebanese Christians and Druse. Syria continued to maintain a strong military position in Lebanon, and it became increasingly clear that Israel's original hopes of a compliant Lebanese government were unrealistic. More and more the Gemayel government deferred to

7. Ibid., May 10, 1983.

Damascus, and in March, 1984, repudiated the May 17th Agreement. Nor had the PLO threat been finally exorcised. Despite the departure of the bulk of its forces from Lebanon (under U.S. auspices), the PLO was still capable of launching terrorist attacks inside Israel. Resistance to the Israeli occupation in the West Bank and Gaza remained strong. The dubiety of Israel's goals in the Lebanese war was increasingly the subject of public debate in Israel.

Simultaneously there occurred a marked deterioration in the Israeli economy. The series of tax cuts, especially on consumer goods, instituted by Finance Minister Aridor prior to the 1981 election, had resulted in highly adverse consequences for Israel's trade balance, which in 1983 was expected to show a deficit of $5 billion. In early 1983 there remained only three months of cash reserves. Most foreign aid was used by the Government to pay Government debts, with debt service increasing to 32 percent of export earnings. The total foreign debt amounted by midyear to $21 billion. Inflation soared beyond the previous high of 130 percent a year.

In August the Government took belated steps to shore up the economy. Aridor became a late convert to a drastic austerity program. The Israeli shekel was devalued by 7.5 percent to curb imports, but consumer buying of foreign goods persisted at a high level. After acrimonious discussions the Cabinet voted drastic reductions in public spending amounting to $700 million. Aridor's proposed cuts in social services and defense expenditures met strong opposition in the Cabinet. His critics said the cut of $135 million in education would effectively end Israel's system of free secondary education. Due to intensive efforts by Defense Minister Arens, the initial proposal of a $360 million reduction in military appropriations was scaled down by $60 million.

Prior to the Sabra and Shatilla massacres the Likud government enjoyed a public approval rating of 66 percent. By early 1983 the Government's rating had dropped to 44 percent, and by midyear the Likud and Labor parties were running virtually even in preference polls.(8) Many observers voiced doubt that the Likud government would survive until the expiry of its mandate in 1985.

The Resignation of Prime Minister Begin and Formation of the Shamir Government

Late in August, 1983, a dispirited Begin shocked his Cabinet colleagues by abruptly announcing his imminent resignation. "I cannot go on," Begin confessed, insisting that his decision was irrevocable. Personal problems--grief over his wife's death and his own poor health, were considered an important factor in Begin's resignation. But his disappointment over the unimpressive results and heavy losses incurred in the Lebanese war and the steadily worsening state of the economy also appeared to be significant factors.

Begin's departure marked the passing of Israel's veteran political generation which emerged in the pre-independence period. The impact of his six-year tenure as Prime Minister was widely debated in Israel. Begin had become the leading symbol of militant Israeli nationalism, the champion of unrestricted Jewish settlement on the West Bank and Gaza and permanent Israeli control over the West Bank. At the same time he was the first Prime Minister to sign a peace treaty with an Arab state. Begin's critics argued that the peace treaty with Egypt in 1979 in fact facilitated Israeli expansion against other Arab states like Lebanon, and in any case was dependent on a friendly regime in Cairo. The Lebanese war, they claimed, had introduced fresh strains in relations with Mubarak's Egypt, and cast doubt on the treaty's future efficacy.

In domestic politics Begin was identified more than any other Israeli leader with the rise of the Oriental Jews as a powerful and potentially deci-

---

8. "Israel: A Time of Retrenchment," Alan Dowty, *Current History* 83, no. 489 (1984): 14.

sive political force in Israeli politics. Largely
untutored in democratic politics, the Oriental
Jews, according to some observers, could move
Israel in the direction of an authoritarian political system. In the sweeping concessions he made
to his religious party cohorts in the coalitions
formed in 1977 and 1981, Begin appeared to have
altered the religious status quo by tilting the
precarious balance between the secularists and the
religious in favor of the latter. Finally Begin's
fulsome support of Jewish settlements in the West
Bank and Gaza after 1977 increased the probability
of their formal annexation by Israel.(9)

The immediate impact of Begin's resignation was
to reactivate the leadership succession struggle
in his Herut party. Foreign Minister Shamir and
Deputy Prime Minister Levy emerged as the chief
contenders. Sharon unexpectedly withdrew his
candidacy in favor of Shamir. Shamir enjoyed
several advantages over Levy, who was considered
inexperienced in foreign and military affairs.
Shamir had the backing of the influential Herut
old guard, and despite Levy's Moroccan origins,
some support from Oriental Jews. At Levy's insistence the choice of party leader was made by the
930-member Herut central committee. In a secret
ballot vote on September 2, Shamir won over Levy,
436-302.(10)

The negotiations for a new government proved
difficult. With the Likud bloc controlling only
46 votes in the Knesset, minor parties in the old
coalition were in a strong position to extract
fresh concessions. The Tami party, with three
seats, demanded the restoration of recent budget

9. See Meron Benvenisti's *The West Bank Data Project: A Survey of
Israel's Policies*. (Washington, D.C.: American Enterprise Institute, 1984), pp. 59-60.

10. Born in eastern Poland in 1915, Shamir emigrated to Palestine
in 1935 and was leader of the Stern Gang, a splinter off Begin's
Irgun. After independence, Shamir served in the secret intelligence service (Mossad) until 1965, joined Begin's Herut party in
1970, and entered the Knesset in 1973, where he became Speaker in
1977. Before his appointment as Foreign Minister in 1980, he opposed the Camp David accords.

cuts in the social services. The ultraorthodox Agudat, with four seats, renewed its demand for legislation to ban archeological digs on religious sites and restrict conversions to Judaism to Orthodox rabbis for registration purposes. Although these matters were covered in the 1981 Coalition Agreement, promised legislative action had not ensued.

A new complication was introduced, when four Liberal party members of the Likud bloc and two independents--Ben-Porat and Hurvitz, insisted that the Likud leadership make serious efforts to form a national unity government with the opposition Labor party. After ten days of backroom negotiations conducted by Levy, the old coalition parties agreed to form a new government based on their 1981 accord. This paved the way for the required formal steps to be taken by President Herzog.

At the outset Herzog turned down a bid by the Labor party, which held 50 Knesset seats, to initiate its own coalition talks. Following consultations with the lesser parties, he asked Shamir to form a new government September 21. In the unity talks to which Shamir agreed, the Labor party spokesmen made its participation conditional on the adoption of three policies: speedy withdrawal from Lebanon, a halt in the Likud's settlement policies on the West Bank and Gaza and an effort to bring Jordan's King Hussein into peace negotiations. The talks broke down September 30. According to Shamir they collapsed because Labor "wanted Likud to form a government to implement Labor policies."

After another round of talks with Agudat representatives, Shamir won Knesset approval for his government (the old Begin six-party coalition comprised of the Herut, Liberal, La'am, Tehiya, Tami, NRP and Agudat parties) by a close vote of 60-53. Mr. Begin absented himself from the Knesset vote. Shamir retained his post as Foreign Minister as well as taking over the prime ministership.(11) In his Knesset speech Shamir pledged

11. Levy later charged that Shamir had blocked his appointment as Foreign Minister.

to continue Begin's foreign policy and carry out the "sacred work" of settling the West Bank and Gaza, but warned of stormy economic weather ahead.

A severe economic crisis had already erupted. Fearful of further devaluation, many Israelis had been buying U.S. dollars and other foreign currencies. The value of Israeli bank shares began to plummet, when a large number of shareholders cashed them in to purchase dollars. Within two days in early October an estimated $26 million in dollars were purchased. The commercial banks insisted the Government take emergency action. On October 9 the Tel Aviv stock exchange was closed to avoid panic selling, and all sales of foreign currency were halted. Two days later the Government announced several ameliorative steps. The shekel was devalued by over 18 percent, which coupled with devaluation by the banks, represented a total devaluation of more than 23 percent. The Government agreed to introduce legislation to insure the value of bank shares for a five-year period. Government spending was to be cut an additional five percent. Commodity subsidies were reduced, leading to a substantial increase in food and fuel prices. Aridor insisted the new subsidy cuts not be covered by the usual automatic cost-of-living increases for workers, which immediately provoked a two-hour general strike, instigated by the Histadrut, by a million workers.

Aridor's next step was to advance the astonishing proposal that the Israeli shekel be directly linked to the American dollar. He claimed the "dollarization" of the economy would enable Israel to reduce its inflationary rate to a two-figure level within a short period. His plan created a national uproar. Spokesmen on both the left and the right denounced his scheme as an intolerable compromising of Israeli sovereignty and national honor. Aridor immediately resigned, and Prime Minister Shamir hastened to explain the Cabinet had never seriously entertained Aridor's proposal. Yigal Cohen-Orgad, an economist and business consultant, was named Aridor's successor as Finance Minister.

Budgetary Dislocations and Likud Defections

Cabinet discussions early in 1984 on the Government's budget for 1984-85 revealed serious
divisions in the Likud coalition. Tami's Minister
of Labor and Social Welfare, Aharon Uzan, attacked
the proposed cuts in social spending, stating that
an increase of six percent was required rather
than the proposed six percent reduction. Tami
spokesmen hinted they might leave the Government
coalition in the near future. Finance Minister
Cohen-Orgad argued for a one-year freeze in West
Bank settlements. Settler committees immediately
complained that only $200 million out of a total
$250 million appropriation in the previous year's
budget had actually been spent, and that only
1,800 out of 4,000 projected housing units for
prospective settlers had been constructed. Prime
Minister Shamir remained adamantly opposed to any
cutback in the Government's settlement program.
Defense Minister Arens was so incensed by proposed
cuts in his department, he threatened to resign.
Agreement on the budget was reached only after
Shamir himself stated he would resign, unless all
departments accepted an overall nine percent reduction.

In February the Knesset approved a budget of
nearly $23 billion, of which two-thirds was ab-
sorbed by debt servicing and defense expenditures.
It increased health charges, introduced a fee
system in secondary education and provided for a
reduction in imports. Cohen-Orgad warned that
Israeli living standards must revert to 1982
levels. An increase in unemployment from two to
six and one-half percent was predicted. Simultaneously the Government announced a new round of
price increases and restrictions both on foreign
currency transactions and investment in foreign
securities.

A showdown on the question of early elections--
more than a year ahead of schedule, occurred in
March. Aharon Abuhatzeira, head of the three-man
Tami faction, announced that his party was leaving
the Likud coalition and would sponsor a bill call-

ing for a new election. He argued that recourse to the electorate was necessitated by the country's desperate economic situation with inflation having increased to about 300 percent a year. Two other Government supporters--Liberal party maverick, Yitzhak Berman, and independent Ben-Porat, who had resigned his Cabinet post two months earlier, indicated they would join the Tami MKs in voting for early elections.

In rebuttal Prime Minister Shamir argued that more time was required for the Government's recently adopted austerity program to show results. Facing defeat in the Knesset, Shamir called for a secret ballot on the election bill. He was hopeful that a few Labor party members who might not secure a safe seat on their party's list at the next election, would oppose an early election, if they could vote anonymously. But Knesset Speaker Menahem Savidor ruled against a secret ballot and in favor of a vote by show of hands. With five Likud defectors the measure passed 61-58. Mr. Begin again absented himself.

It was left to Shamir and Labor party leader Peres, to negotiate the actual election date. Peres favored an early election, so that his party could capitalize on Likud's declining position in opinion polls. Shamir wanted a much later date to give him time to stabilize his Government and attempt to improve the economy. After prolonged discussion they agreed on July 23, which the Knesset approved.

(2) The Campaign

Compared to the tumultuous electoral campaign in 1981, the 1984 campaign seemed a lackluster effort. The dynamic presence of Menachem Begin was missing. His successor Shamir, was a colorless figure on the campaign trail. Shimon Peres was stolid as always. Only at the rallies held by Ariel Sharon were there echoes of the old Beginite brouhaha. Interparty confrontations between the Likud and Labor were infrequent. The Labor party, anticipating victory, played it safe. The "clean election" pact, engineered by the Central Election Commission, helped reduce the high level of campaign violence, which had characterized the 1981 campaign. The calamitous state of the economy proved a less compelling issue than anticipated. The chances of an early withdrawal of Israeli troops from Lebanon and the well-worn issue of Jewish settlements on the West Bank attracted some voter attention. Acute factional rivalries within the Likud and the religious bloc absorbed much of their leaders' energies. The external environment remained calm, preventing the incumbent Likud government from exploiting foreign developments as in 1981. Voter apathy was pronounced.

Leadership Selection in the Herut and Labor Parties

At the outset of the campaign Prime Minister Shamir was confronted with a serious challenge. Deputy Prime Minister Levy, whom Shamir had earlier defeated for party leader, weighed the advisability of a second challenge. After some equivocation he decided not to enter the contest. Levy claimed he acted in the interests of party unity and to prevent any "lingering bitterness" in party circles.(12) If Levy had suffered a second defeat at Shamir's hands, as most observers predicted, it would have damaged his chances for future party preferment. Shamir shortly named Levy to head the Likud's election campaign.

Unwilling to follow Levy's example, General Sharon carried his challenge of the Herut central committee in early April. He made a surprisingly good showing, winning 42.2 percent of the vote. Shamir got 407 votes (56 percent) out of 725 ballots, Sharon 306 votes. Sharon had been expected to win only between 10 and 20 percent of the vote. For the first time in its history the Herut was headed by a leader who did not have

12. *Jerusalem Post, International Edition*, April 16, 1984.

overwhelming support of its membership. Sharon had radically improved his own position in the Herut leadership, not only staking out a claim for a senior cabinet position, should the Likud win the election, but also enhancing his prospects in future party elections.

For the first time in a decade the Labor party avoided a divisive fight over Party leader. In 1983 when Yitzhak Navon had retired as Israel's President, many Labor party members favored him as successor to Shimon Peres, who had led Labor to two successive defeats. As an Oriental Jew (a category in short supply in the Labor leadership) and popular former President, Navon was seen as an ideal leader to retrieve Labor party fortunes. Former Premier Rabin, Peres' arch rival, was also expected to make another run for the party's top post. Surprisingly neither Navon nor Rabin opposed Peres, who was unanimously endorsed by Labor's central committee. When the three leaders appeared together before the committee, an effusive Peres said they were "a threesome who are seeking to do battle together and not with each other."(13)

Slate-Making Problems in the Likud and Labor Blocs

For a brief period the 19-year alliance between the Herut and Liberal parties seemed threatened by an abrupt dissolution. In 1965 the two somewhat unequal partners--Herut was acknowledged to be the stronger, had agreed that the Liberals would be allocated 15 of the first 40 seats in their combined electoral list. Since the Likud victory in 1977, Herut leaders had become increasingly impatient with what they regarded as the Liberals' disproportionate number of safe Knesset seats.

Pre-election negotiations to revise the 1965 agreement proved stormy. The Herut team insisted that the Liberals' current representation in the Knesset be reduced from 18 to 12 seats, and a full

13. *Jerusalem Post, International Edition*, April 8, 1984.

merger of the two parties be formalized before the election in July. The Liberal party leadership was divided between the pragmatists willing to concede some reduction in their representation, and those willing to risk an independent slate. In the view of some Herut members, the latter alternative would make the Liberals a small, uninfluential parliamentary party. Yitzhak Modai, the Liberal party chairman who took over the major negotiating role, indicated a marked ambivalence between these two positions. At a critical point after signing an agreement with Herut, he abruptly shifted course and said the Liberals were prepared to go it alone. Under the aegis of Herut leader Shamir, the two allies worked out an arrangement shortly before the filing deadline for party lists. The Liberals agreed to reduced representation, but the proposed merger was postponed indefinitely. In a close election Herut was reluctant to lose votes which the Liberals supplied the bloc.

Shamir's intervention was also required to settle a contest between two contenders for leadership of the small La'am faction, and arrange reduction of its numbers of safe seats to three, compared to the four won by La'am in the 1981 election. After the election La'am was expected to merge with Herut.

In the Herut central committee's vote on the ranking of the top eight Knesset candidates, Sharon suffered another setback. He ran against David Levy for the party's No. 2 slot, which Sharon believed would help him regain the Defense Ministry, should the Likud win the election. Levy decided he would not cut a deal with Sharon and back out of the contest. Shamir announced that if the Likud won the election, he would not allocate cabinet portfolios on the basis of "party popularity contests." In the voting Sharon had to settle for the No. 4 slot, behind both Levy and Defense Minister Arens, who was No. 3. Two Levy supporters also placed within the first eight, further strengthening Levy's position in the party leadership.

In the Labor alignment doubt arose whether the 15-year alliance between the Labor and Mapam parties would be preserved. When two Likud MKs (Yitzhak Peretz and Amnon Linn) crossed the Knesset floor in 1982 and joined Labor, they were promised safe slots on the Alignment list in the next election. Some reshuffling of safe seats became necessary. Victor Shemtov, Mapam's secretary-general, was asked by Labor party leaders to accept seventh, rather than his usual fifth, place on the Alignment list. As a result, Mapam would suffer the loss of one of its seven seats, which it had won in the 1981 election. Initially the Mapam leadership refused to alter its 1969 agreement with Labor. Later the negotiating teams of the two parties agreed that Shemtov would be assigned the No. 7 position, allowing Labor's Abba Eban to take over the No. 5 slot and avoid a rupture in Alignment ranks.

As in 1981 the controlling voice in determining the Labor party's candidate rankings was a four-man committee, this time composed of Peres, Navon, Rabin and Haim Bar-Lev, the party's secretary-general. The four leaders chose half the party's list and then ranked their choices along with the names submitted by the party branches. Most of the latter were assigned less safe seats, while most holders of the safe seats were choices of the four party leaders. The party's central committee approved the entire list.

Party leader Peres was placed in a difficult situation, when he attempted to designate his prospective cabinet members. Two party leaders-- Yitzhak Navon and Abba Eban, were considered for the post of Foreign Minister-designate. Eban had been the nominee in the 1981 election. Peres opted for Navon, claiming that Navon's position as No. 2 on the party list warranted his choice. To placate the disaffected Eban, Peres promised to consider him for a deputy prime ministership and special information post dealing with foreign policy matters.(14)

14. *Jerusalem Post*, May 30, 1984.

Of the 26 parties that filed electoral lists on May 31, ten were new entrants. Four of these require special mention: Ezer Weizman's new centrist party; two new religious parties that were offshoots of established religious parties--the NRP and the Agudat Yisrael; and a new dovish party on the far left with mixed Jewish and Arab leadership--the Progressive List for Peace.

Weizman's party. The new *Yahad* (Together) party was essentially the personal vehicle of its founder, Ezer Weizman--one-time dashing commander of the Israeli Air Force, organizer of the 1977 Likud victory and Defense Minister in the first Begin government, who helped the Prime Minister make a peace treaty with Egypt. Since his resignation as Defense Minister in 1980 and expulsion from the Herut party, Weizman had been intent on staging a political comeback. In organizing the Yahad party, he hoped to win enough Knesset seats in a close election, so he might hold the balance of power between the two major parties and regain a Cabinet seat. His major strategy was to attract disaffected Likud voters.

In Weizman's view Israel was faced with its gravest leadership crisis. With his former colleagues in the Likud everything had turned sour, he claimed--"peace, the economy, social unity and religion." Fresh leadership that could "awaken hope and plant the feeling of confidence" deserved the highest priority. The "right leader at the right place at the right time" could, he argued, make a significant difference in "finding solutions to the toughest problems."(15)

Foreign policy and security issues were stressed in Weizman's campaign. He favored an accelerated and ultimately total withdrawal of Israeli forces from Lebanon. He charged that the Camp David peace process had become a "shadow" of its "original aspirations" and committed himself to its revival, if he were part of the next govern-

15. *Jerusalem Post, International Edition*, March 25, 1984.

ment. Weizman called for direct talks with Jordan and Syria which would include representatives of the PLO. A special feature of Weizman's campaign was his attracting large, friendly crowds in several Arab towns.

Weizman received important organization support from several of his former colleagues in the IDF. General Benyamin Ben-Eliezer resigned as coordinator of civilian activities in the occupied territories to accept the No. 2 slot on the Yahad electoral list. Weizman's successor as Air Force commander, General Mordechai Hod, was given the No. 4 position, and another ex-Air Force officer, No. 8. Also included in the top ten of the Yahad list were an Oriental Jew and an Arab, both town councillors, a Haifa University professor and a woman director of a construction company. But like General Dayan in the 1981 election, Weizman's expectations of mobilizing mass support never materialized.

Fissures in the religious camp. In the 1984 election there was a four-way division in the bloc of religious parties: the NRP, the Agudat, and the two new groups--the *Morasha* party and the Sephardi Tora Guardians, known as *Shas*, all sponsoring separate electoral lists.

The Morasha party was an electoral alliance of the *Matzad* party (Rally of Religious Zionists) and Poali Agudat Yisrael worker's party (PAY). The Matzad party was organized in February, 1983, by NRP rightwingers, led by Rabbi Haim Druckman. The NRP split arose over differences on Israel's withdrawal from the Sinai peninsula under the 1979 peace treaty with Egypt. Druckman's faction was strongly opposed to any territorial concession by Israel to an Arab state. In allying with the PAY party, Druckman's party expected to attract both NRP and Agudat defectors. Like its secular counterpart, the Tehiya party, Morasha was essentially a single-issue party--unimpeded Jewish settlements in the occupied territories and no withdrawal by Israel.

The emergence of the Shas party represented a rejection of the predominantly Ashkenazi leader-snip of the ultraorthodox Agudat party by a sizable bloc of pious Oriental Jews. The Council of Sages, the Agudat's governing body, had no Oriental members. All four of Agudat's Knesset seats were held by Ashkenazim. Many Oriental parents had been persuaded to send their children to Agudat-run schools, which had mostly Ashkenazim faculties. The bulk of Government funds for religious institutions under the Agudat went to Ashkenazim bodies. The organization of Shas in 1983 was intended to redress these cumulative grievances.

Under the leadership of a young rabbi, Nissim Ze'ev, the new party had won three seats in 1983, the same as the established Agudat party, on the Jerusalem municipal council of 21 members. The new Shas party was viewed as a serious threat to Abuhatzeira's Tami party, also a predominantly Oriental party, but with a more secular orientation.

Already weakened by factional secessions, the NRP and Agudat parties were plagued by internal disputes over placements on their respective electoral lists.

In the NRP the long-time leaders of the Young Guard faction, Minister of Education Zevulun Hammer and MK Yehuda Ben-Meir, took the preliminary step of filing as an independent list. A parliamentary committee had authorized them to act as a separate Knesset faction, which entitled them to Government campaign financing at the NRP's expense and also waived the requirement of an electoral deposit. In meetings with other NRP factional leaders, Hammer and Ben-Meir lobbied for giving Oriental Jews the third and fourth places on the NRP list, and insisted that one or more non-political personalities be included in order to enhance the NRP's electoral appeal.

Last-minute talks prior to the filing deadline between Hammer and Yosef Burg, leader of the Lamifne faction, led to a compromise agreement. Professor Avner Sciaky of the Tel Aviv University law school faculty, an Oriental Jew proposed by Hammer as a "non-political personality," was given the

No. 3 slot, behind Burg and Hammer. An Oriental
member of Burg's faction, David Danino, was assigned the No. 4 position. Ben-Meir got the No. 7
slot. At a stormy meeting of the NRP executive
committee, the list was approved amid shouted
protests by some Oriental members that they were
being used to "decorate" the list.(16) The Emunah
religious women's faction raised objections to its
assignment to the No. 8 position, and decided to
run an independent list. Later, however, the
Emunah faction returned to the NRP fold.

A heated controversy arose in the Agudat party
over a proposal by its governing body, the Council
of Sages, that no Agudat MK who had served two
terms or more would be eligible for re-election.
Veteran MK's Shlomo Lorincz and Menahem Porush
(members of the so-called "Lithuanian" faction)
refused to retire. After acrimonious discussions
by rival factions, a compromise agreement was
reached. MK Lorincz would be retired, but Porush
was assigned the important No. 2 slot on the
Agudat list. In a novel rotation arrangment it
was provided that the first ten candidates on the
Agudat list would deposit with the Council of
Sages letters of resignation from the Knesset,
dated two years after the convening of the 11th
Knesset. The Council would subsequently decide
which letters to activate.

Porush's candidacy for the No. 2 position was
strongly opposed by factional supporters of the
Gur Rabbi, Simcha Bunin. On June 2 a group of
about 50 Hasidics raided Rabbi Porush's synagogue
in Jerusalem, assaulted him and other worshippers.
Porush had to be hospitalized. Porush's attackers
were later identified as members of the Hasidic
Gur faction.

New Leftist Party. The Progressive List for
Peace (PLP) represented an electoral coalition of
several Israeli Arab nationalists and a number of
well-known Jewish leftists. It was headed by an
Arab nationalist, Mohammed Miari, a lawyer from
Haifa. Uri Avnery, a maverick former MK, and

16. *Jerusalem Post, International Edition,* June 3, 1984.

156

General Matti Peled, both long identified with the Israeli peace movement, were the leading Jewish members.

There were several forerunners to the PLP, the most important being the Arab al-Ard movement in the 1960s. Al-Ard represented a threat to the Government's established policy of dividing the Arab electorate by encouraging particularistic clan and village interests in the Arab sector. It was declared illegal under the Emergency Regulations and later barred by the Supreme Court from presenting a list of candidates for election to the Knesset. In 1972 an organization called the Heads of Arab Local Councils was set up, which was supposed to confine itself to local matters. This restriction was modifed, when Prime Minister Rabin met with this group and discussed national issues.

The staging of the Land Day mass demonstrations in 1976 represented a potentially formidable Arab organization. The PLP's Miari claimed that in 1984 Israel Arabs were taking "all the political forces into account," and that a joint electoral effort with dovish Jews represented "progress" for the Arab cause.(17) The PLP was based on the organizational principle of absolute Jewish-Arab parity, and on its electoral list Arab candidates alternated with Jewish candidates. Miari was, for example, assigned the No. 1 position on the party list, and General Peled the No. 2 slot.

The PLP provided formidable competition for the Communist Rakah party and its Democratic Front, which had previously won the largest segment of the Israeli Arab vote. For Arabs who disliked Rakah's Moscow connection, the PLP offered a welcome option. Both the PLP and Rakah favored the establishment of an independent Palestine state, and both sought the PLO's endorsement. Rakah claimed that the PLO's National Council had supported Rakah since 1976. A PLO newspaper in Cyprus was quoted by PLP leaders to demonstrate the PLO's preference for the Progressive List.

17. See Yosef Goell's interview with Miari, *Jerusalem Post, International Edition*, July 15, 1984.

Enter General Eytan. An important new partici-
pant was the rightist *Tzomet* movement, organized
by the IDF´s forceful former Chief of Staff, Rafael Eytan, who retired shortly after having been
censured by the Kahan Commission (see above).
Early in the campaign Eytan merged his movement
with the ultranationalist Tehiya party.

General Eytan is another significant example of
an Israeli military hero turned politician. He
became nationally prominent in the Yom Kippur War,
when he played a major role in turning the tide on
the Golan Heights in Israel´s favor. Appointed by
the Likud government in 1978, Eytan was a highly
political Chief of Staff. Incoming IDF recruits
were seen by him as proper subjects of indoctrina-
tion in nationalist ideology. Eytan´s bluntly
articulated views in the Israeli media proved
highly controversial. In an Independence Day
interview on Israel TV in 1978, he said Israelis
"should stop being naive" about their country´s
security needs and intentions of the Arabs, who,
he claimed, were using political negotiations as
"another means" of obliterating Israel.(18) In
two instances General Eytan substantially reduced
heavy sentences earlier imposed by military
courts, one involving an IDF reservist for murder-
ing a Jerusalem Arab and in a second case, an IDF
officer convicted of a manslaughter charge in
Lebanon. Negative public reaction was considerable in 1983, when General Eytan compared young
Arab stone-throwers against Jewish settlers to
"drugged cockroaches running about hither and
thither in a bottle."(19) As Chief of Staff,
Eytan was known to be sympathetic to Gush Emunim
squatters in the West Bank.

General Eytan´s entry in the political arena
created a stir. Once having joined with Tehiya,
he succeeded in winning the No. 2 slot on their
combined electoral list behind Science Minister
Ne´eman. MK Guela Cohen grudgingly accepted the
No. 3 position, a marginally safe seat, after she

18. *Jerusalem Post, International Edition,* August 19, 1984.

19. Ibid.

had threatened to bolt the party, if she were assigned a lower position.

Eytan's insistence in campaign speeches that Israeli Arabs should enjoy full civil rights only if they performed national service aroused critical comment. Pre-election polls showed that Eytan's candidacy substantially improved Tehiya's chances, and would probably make it Israel's third largest party.

In every Knesset election there are a number of miniscule, essentially single-man parties, which in a few cases have responsible leadership and receive serious attention. In 1984 there were three: (1)the center-rightist *Ometz* (Courage to Cure the Economy) party, led by the Finance Minister of the first Begin government (Hurvitz), an advocate of economic austerity; (2)the dovish list of Arieh Eliav, veteran ex-Labor party leader and former leader of the defunct Shelli party; and (3)Mordachai Ben-Porat, former member of the Likud government, who called his party "The Movement for Revival." If one or more of these prominent politicians passed the one percent threshold, they could expect to play a marginal role in coalition formation.

The Question of Banning Extremist Parties

In only one previous case had the Israeli Supreme Court ruled a political party illegal--the al-Ard party in 1965. In 1984 the Court was presented with two cases of parties representing opposite poles in the political spectrum--Rabbi Kahane's Kach party on the extreme right and the leftist, pro-Arab PLP. Earlier the Israeli security services had advised Defense Minister Moshe Arens that he declare the PLP an illegal organization on grounds of its alleged subversiveness. Surprisingly Arens refused to invoke the Emergency Regulations against the PLP. But subsequently the Central Election Commission, comprised of representatives of the leading parties, voted to ban both Kach and the PLP.

The commission first took action against the extremist Kach party, which advocated wholesale expulsion of Israeli Arabs. Voting in favor of the ban were delegates of the center-left parties--the Alignment, Shinui, CRM and Rakah. The rightist-nationalist parties--Tehiya, Tami, NRP, Agudat and some Likud members, opposed it. Other Likud members accounted for seven abstentions. The commission held the Kach party should be banned, because it "advocated racist and anti-democratic principles" and "openly supported terror." In the majority view Kach was responsible for "fanning hatred among various segments of the population."(20)

A second party division marked the commission's vote to disqualify the leftist PLP--with 17 votes in favor, 12 opposed and four abstentions. Although most Alignment members opposed the ban, three abstained. Uri Avnery, co-chairman of the PLP, later charged that the ban was a "scandalous plot, which the Likud and the Alignment hatched between them" to disqualify the PLP.(21) In banning the PLP, the commission held that the party included "subversive elements" and that "key persons on the list" were identified with "enemies of the state."

In late June the five-man Supreme Court voted unanimously to reverse the commission's ban on the two parties, clearing the way for their inclusion on the July 23 ballot.

Campaign Strategies and Issues

At the outset of the campaign the Labor party adopted a deliberately low-keyed "soft" strategy, designed to attract wavering Likud supporters. Party strategists claimed that as many as 60 percent of Likud voters were undecided as to their

20. *Jerusalem Post, International Edition*, June 24, 1984.

21. *Jerusalem Post, International Edition*, July 2, 1984.

voting preference in 1984. Confrontational tactics were to be avoided, relatively few large street rallies were planned and differences with the Likud over issues blurred. Labor's campaign manager, one-time IDF Chief of Staff Mordechai Gur, announced that Labor's major target areas were voters in urban centers, especially in working class districts, and development towns, both considered Likud strongholds.(22) As a hopeful augury, Gur cited a five percent swing to Labor in recent municipal elections. Labor campaigners would, he said, criticize Likud policies, but selectively, "without emotion," and avoid personal attacks on Government leaders. Former Likud voters would not, it was assumed, want to listen to blanket criticism of views they once held.

Implementation of Labor's strategy caused considerable frustration in the Likud camp. Their campaign chief, David Levy, complained: "Where are the Labor people hiding? Have they taken refuge in a Trappist monastery, and taken vows of silence?"(23) Another Likud spokesman claimed that Labor was trying to "tranquilize" the campaign and undercut the Likud's effort to bring out a large vote, considered favorable to the Likud.

The Likud faced an uphill struggle. Opinion polls predicted a Labor party victory, in some cases by more than ten percent. The severe economic crisis continued without abatement. There were new casualties in occupied southern Lebanon. In the first phase of the campaign Likud leaders were preoccupied with internal factional problems.

Thrown on the defensive, the Likud sought to stress what it regarded as positive features in its spotty seven-year record: an improved standard of living, which despite high inflation, most Israelis were said to enjoy; the success of its "ethnic revolution," which the Likud claimed had restored the Orientals' sense of pride, making them feel for the first time equal members in Israeli society; the continuously expanding Jewish

22. *Jerusalem Post, International Edition,* April 22, 1984.

23. *Jerusalem Post, International Edition,* June 24, 1984.

settlement program on the West Bank; and consistent support for an enlarged Eretz Israel.

Three issues dominated the campaign: the state of the economy; the future of Jewish settlements on the West Bank; and Israel's relations with Lebanon.

The economic issue. Predictably the Labor party attempted to exploit Likud's highly vulnerable economic performance. In the nine months since Shamir had become Prime Minister, Israel's inflationary rate had doubled from 200 to 400 percent. Foreign currency reserves were dangerously low. National insolvency appeared imminent. A Labor-led government would drastically reduce inflation in one year and take three steps to cut Government expenditures by one billion dollars: (1)freeze Jewish settlements in "non-essential" areas in the occupied territories; (2)withdraw Israeli troops from Lebanon; and (3)reduce payments to institutions controlled by the religious parties.(24) Labor promised to increase Israel's gross national product by $8 billion in five years and simultaneously reduce the balance-of-payments deficit. A Labor government would give preference to the industrial sector, especially export-oriented firms. To reduce inflation, Labor advocated a comprehensive agreement between Histadrut and private employers.

In defense of its record the Likud pointed to Israel's low level of unemployment, the impact of wage-indexing in ameliorating the high level of inflation, Government's heavy investment in industrial infrastructure and the benefits of its Project Renewal in urban neighborhoods. The new austerity program undertaken by Finance Minister Cohen-Orgad would, it was argued, lead to economic recovery in the near future.

Jewish settlements and the future of the West Bank. Labor leader Peres said he would halt construction of Jewish settlements near densely populated Arab areas, and open talks with Jordan's

---

24. See the statement by the head of Labor's economic team, Gad Yaacobi, *Jerusalem Post, International Edition,* June 24, 1984.

King Hussein and moderate Palestinians on the
future of the West Bank. Negotiations with Jordan
would be based either on United Nations resolu-
tions 242 and 338 or with no prior conditions on
either side. A significant difference in Labor's
1984 platform from previous declarations was that
no explicit reference was made to territorial
compromise on the Golan Heights. Peres said he
saw no realistic possibility of negotiations with
Syria on Golan in the foreseeable future. Labor
promised that no settlements in the occupied territories would be dismantled by a Labor government.

The Likud insisted, however, that Labor intended to make a deal with the Arabs and "sell
out" Jewish settlers on the West Bank. Prime
Minister Shamir claimed that King Hussein was not
interested in serious negotiations with Israel.
Peres interjected that Shamir inconsistently depicted Hussein as intending to negotiate with a
Labor government. In contrast to Labor's position
favoring territorial concessions on the West Bank,
Shamir insisted the Likud would never relinquish
Israeli control over the West Bank and Gaza. To
maximize what the Likud viewed as its advantage
over Labor on the settlements issue, the Government announced in early July immediate construction of eight new West Bank settlements, and
shortly before the election the Cabinet approved
five more.

The Lebanon question. Israel's occupation of
southern Lebanon was estimated to cost more than
one million dollars a day and since Israel's withdrawal south of the Awali River in 1983, had
claimed the lives of more than 70 Israelis with
nearly 400 wounded. While both parties favored an
Israeli withdrawal, they disagreed on its timing.

Peres indicated that a Labor government would
attempt to arrange a withdrawal "within three to
six months."(25) Under Labor's policy of "portable
defense," southern Lebanon was seen as a "flexible
area of maneuvering." Israel would set up an

25. Ibid.

early warning system in southern Lebanon and also rely on aerial surveillance, Peres said.

For the Likud Shamir said that he could not "set timetables" for withdrawal from Lebanon. Such an action would be feasible only when Israel's northern border was secure. His government was pledged to support the strengthening of the pro-Israel South Lebanon Army under General Antoine Lahad, successor to the Haddad militia, which Shamir claimed was already increasing the amount of Lebanese territory under its control. The difference in the two parties' position on the Lebanon question appeared marginal with each party hedging its future actions.

During the campaign two political advertisements published under Likud auspices caused a heated exchange with Labor. One ad featured Likud's recently adopted slogan, "We Are in the National Camp." Labor complained that the ad was intended to divide the nation and incite voters against Labor. When the Likud responded by substituting an ad with the slogan, "One Israel-One Nation," the Labor party ran full-page ads, congratulating the Likud for having "finally rejoined the nation," and calling the division of the nation into camps a "national disaster."(26) The Labor party was also outraged, when a pro-Likud citizens group sponsored an ad featuring a picture of King Hussein and stating, "He (Hussein) wants the (Labor) Alignment." In the same ad the PLO's Yasir Arafat was linked with Hussein's alleged endorsement of Labor.

In the last days of the campaign the Likud, still lagging in the opinion polls, shifted course. Prime Minister Shamir made repeated calls for formation of a national unity government with the opposition Labor party. As Israel's economic crisis persisted, an increasing number of Israelis looked with favor on a unity government. The Likud's new strategy was intended to discourage large-scale defections of Likud voters to Labor. If Labor could be induced to join forces with

26. Ibid.

Likud in a post-election coalition, the wavering Likud voters would presumably be less motivated to desert their party. Labor's Peres rejected Shamir's bid, calling it "election propaganda."

The Trial of the Jewish Terrorists

In June the opening of the trial of 22 Israelis accused of terrorist acts against Arabs on the West Bank raised the controversial territorial question in stark form. The accused represented a group of deeply religious, well-educated Israelis, some of whom were IDF officers and military heroes and had close connections to the Land of Israel and Gush Emunim movements. They were charged with having formed an anti-Arab terrorist group after six Jewish worshippers were murdered in Hebron in April, 1980. The group was alleged to have carried out several major crimes: the planting of car-bombs that crippled two West Bank mayors in 1980--Bassam Shaka of Nablus and Karim Khalaf of Ramallah; a machine gun and grenade attack at Islamic University in Hebron in July 1983, which killed three students and wounded 33; the rigging of bombs in April that could have blown up five crowded Arab buses--the incident that precipitated Government action against the group; and a plot to destroy the Muslim shrine on Temple Mount in Jerusalem.(27) An electronics engineer and IDF reserve officer from Kiryat Arba, Menachem Livni, was cited as leader of the conspiracy. Included among the defendants were the secretary-general of Gush Emunim, a former deputy chairman of the Kiryat Arba settlement council, a founder of the Ofra settlement and a West Bank land broker. Two officers in the West Bank military administration later admitted in court that they had been aware of a 1980 bomb plot against the Arab mayor of al-Bireh, but had done nothing to prevent it.

Revelations regarding the terrorist group had immediate repercussions in the electoral campaign.

27. *The Economist* (London), June 2, 1984.

In newspaper interviews leaders of the group strongly criticized the first Begin government for having encouraged Jewish settlements in the West Bank, but failing to protect or provide them with adequate means of self-defence. Ezer Weizman, Defense Minister at the time, was the special target of the group's criticism. Weizman, they claimed, had failed to take effective action against West Bank Arabs who resorted to violence in opposing Israeli-Egyptian talks on Palestinian autonomy.

Public reactions by political leaders were mixed. Science Minister Ne'eman of the ultra-nationalist Tehiya party openly defended the actions of the terrorist group. He drew a sharp distinction between attacks on innocent people which were condemnable, and attacks on the West Bank mayors who, Ne'eman said, had incited Arabs to anti-Jewish violence. A prominent Labor dove (Yossi Sarid) accused Ne'eman of being the terrorists' arm in the Government.(28) Other Labor spokesmen said the climate of feeling generated by the Begin government encouraged the formation of the group and ultimately the excesses of the Lebanese war in 1982. Prime Minister Shamir attempted to play down the importance of the trials, stating that Jewish terrorism represented a "deviation."

Opinion polls indicated that many Israelis were sympathetic to the accused. Although 60 percent of Israelis were flatly opposed to any kind of Jewish terrorist organization, nearly a third thought that attacks on Arabs could be at least partially, if not wholly justified. Over a third of the respondents said that if the 22 accused were found guilty, they should either receive light-to-nominal sentences or be freed.

When the trial of the 22 was recessed until September, there was a subsidence in the electorate's interest. But it raised profound questions regarding the ultimate direction of the settler movement, the dangers of future vigilante actions, the imperatives of Israeli expansionism

28. Ibid.

and the changing character of Israeli democracy.
As for the immediate effect on the electorate,
some observers held that rightist parties, like
Tehiya and Rabbi Kahane's Kach party were the
likeliest beneficiaries.

Diminution in Campaign Violence

In sharp contrast to the turbulent 1981 campaign, there were relatively few violent incidents
in 1984, and these occurred mostly in the last
days of the campaign. In June the Central Election Committee arranged a "clean election" pact
between the two major parties. Both parties promised to adhere to certain guidelines as follows:
(1)no violence, threats or incitement to violence;
(2)no slogans or other remarks referring to a
person's national origin, communal identification
or religious faith; (3)although catcalls were
permissable at rivals' political rallies, disor-
ders at such meetings could not be arranged in
advance; and (4)"degrading caricatures" of political leaders must not be printed or circulated.(29)
More important contributory factors to a relatively calm election were: the absence of Menachem Begin with his vitriolic and provocative
oratorical style; the relegation of the blunt-
spoken Sharon to a secondary role in the campaign;
the inappropriateness of the tone of grievance
that had marked the 1981 campaign, considering the
Likud's claim of a successful "ethnic revolution"
on behalf of Oriental Jews; and Labor's reliance
on a non-confrontational "soft" strategy.

29. *Jerusalem Post, International Edition*, June 17, 1984.

(3)   Election Results

The 1984 election ended in a virtual deadlock
between the two major parties. Labor won 44 Knesset seats, Likud 41. Thirteen smaller parties
qualified for parliamentary seats, eleven entrants
did not. Each of the two major parties won
slightly fewer seats and suffered a decline in
their popular vote. Extremist parties on both the
right and left were strengthened. In the religious camp there was a splintering in the vote with
two new entrants cutting into the previous vote of
the NRP and Agudat. The ethnic factor continued
to be important and took new form in the religious
camp. More than half the Arab vote went to anti-
Zionist parties for the first time. In a somewhat
larger electorate (by nearly 136 thousand), voter
turnout was virtually the same as in 1981--78.7
percent of the eligible voters. (See Table III)

*The diminished electoral strength of Likud and
Labor.* In 1981 the two major parties won nearly
80 percent of Knesset seats; in 1984 this was
reduced to 70 percent. Likud's loss was the
greater. Its record number of 48 seats in 1981
was reduced to 41--a decrease of 14.5 percent.
Likud got 31.9 percent of the popular vote compared to 37.1 in 1981. Labor suffered a loss of
six percent in parliamentary seats--from 47 seats
in 1981 to 44. Its popular vote total was 34.9
percent compared to 36.6 in 1981. Most pre-election polls had predicted the Labor alignment would
gain between 10 and 15 seats. Peres himself had
expected his party to win more than 50 seats and
easily form a new coalition. The trend toward a
two-party system which marked the 1981 election
was not sustained in 1984. The electorate appeared considerably more fragmented.

Likud's losses, although considerable, proved
less than many observers anticipated. As an incumbent party Likud was at the outset of the
campaign faced with several adverse factors: a
deteriorating economy and galloping inflation; the
failure of most of the Government's objectives in

the Lebanese war; loss of its charismatic leader, Menachem Begin, who refused to participate in the electoral campaign; and visible signs of internal stresses in the Likud cabinet. While there were some Likud defectors to more rightist parties, Tehiya-Tzomet and Rabbi Kahane's Kach party, and to Ezer Weizman's centrist Yahad, a solid core of Likud supporters, especially among Oriental voters, remained loyal. The party's close identification with retention of Greater Israel, an expanded program of Jewish settlements in the West Bank and its leaders' coolness to entering serious peace negotiations with Arab states appeared to work in Likud's favor. The living standards of

---

TABLE III

1984 Election Results

Party	Votes	%	Knesset Seats
Labor Alignment	724,074	34.9	44
Likud	661,302	31.9	41
Tehiya	83,037	4.0	5
NRP	73,530	3.5	4
Democratic Front	69,815	3.4	4
Shas	63,605	3.1	4
Shinui	54,747	2.6	3
CRM	49,698	2.4	3
Yahad	46,302	2.2	3
Progressive List for Peace	38,012	1.8	2
Agudat Yisrael	36,079	1.7	2
Morasha	33,287	1.6	2
Tami	31,103	1.5	1
Kach	25,907	1.2	1
Ometz	23,845	1.2	1
Others	58,978	3.0	0
Total	2,073,321	100.0	120

most Israelis had improved in the Begin era, and the Government's recent shift to austerity measures to cope with the mounting economic crisis had not yet imposed severe hardships on Israeli consumers.

Although the Labor alignment was technically the winner, its "victory" was far from decisive. Its non-confrontational campaign strategy of muffling the issues failed to dislodge signficant numbers of Likud voters. Labor's attempt to mute its traditional stand on territorial compromise and assume a more hawkish stance had minimal results. Despite having been the "out" party for seven years, Labor retained its image as the Ashkenazi-dominated Establishmeent for many Oriental voters. Although the Labor leadership was more united than in 1981, Peres was not able to generate a positive response from critically important uncommitted voters. As before, his leadership style was cautious and unexciting. Peres' willingness to agree with Shamir on a July election proved faulty on two grounds. The departure of between 100,000 and 150,000 voters on summer vacation outside Israel at election time included many Labor supporters. Secondly a later election date in November would have allowed more time for negative voter responses to the Likud government's new austerity policies to take effect.

There was a significant 10 percent drop in the Alignment's vote by members of the United Kibbutz movement, long a labor bastion. In 1981 a record 91 percent of UKM members voted Labor. Mrs. Aloni's CRM party was considered the major beneficiary of this shift in 1984.

The strengthening of extremist parties. The election's single most sensational result was the winning of a parliamentary seat by Rabbi Kahane's Kach party for the first time. In 1981 Kach polled a little over five thousand votes. In 1984 its vote was more than five times greater (25,907) and easily passed the one percent threshold. Rabbi Kahane's advocacy of extra-constitutional tactics to attain his primary goal of driving most Arabs out of Israel was certain to cause an uproar

and possibly violent clashes in the Knesset. Kahane's electoral success epitomized and amplified
the rightist trend in Israeli politics since 1967.

The rightist Tehiya-Tzomet party with its tri-
umvirate of highly vocal nationalists--Yuval
Ne'eman, General Eytan and Guela Cohen, significantly increased its electoral support, becoming
the third largest party in the Knesset. Contesting its second election, Tehiya nearly doubled its
vote from 44,677 votes in 1981 to 83,037 in 1984,
an increase of 1.7 percent. The separately
counted soldier's vote gave Tehiya a fifth seat
and reduced the Labor alignment's seats by one, to
44. Gershon Schocken has pointed out that if the
votes of the general electorate had been distributed as were the votes of IDF soldiers (most of
whom were first-time voters), Tehiya would have
had not five, but 14 Knesset seats.(30) Most of
Tehiya's gains came at the Likud's expense. General Eytan, whose views on Israel's Arabs were
similar to Kahane's, helped Tehiya gain fresh
support from younger voters.

On the far left the new pro-Arab Progressive
List for Peace(PLP) made a creditable first showing without cutting into the vote for the Communist Rakah's Democratic Front. With its 38,000
votes the PLP won 1.8 percent of the popular vote
and two parliamentary seats. Competing for virtually the same bloc of Arab votes, the DFPE
received nearly five thousand more votes than in
1981 (a total of 69,815), which, however, represented the same percentage of its popular vote as
in 1981, 3.4 percent. The pro-Arab bloc in the
Knesset now held six seats, four by Rakah's DFPE
and two by the PLP, an increase of two over 1981.

*The splintering of the vote for the religious
parties.* In 1981 the vote for the religious parties was divided between the NRP and the Agudat.
(31) The NRP won six seats with 4.9 percent of

30. "Israel in Election Year 1984," Gershon Schocken, *Foreign
Affairs* 63, no. 1 (1984): 89.

31. In some party classifications Abuhatzeira's Tami Party is included in the religious camp, while in others the Oriental ethnic
base in stressed.

the popular vote; the Agudat four seats with 3.7 percent. In 1984 the vote for the religious parties was split four ways with two new entrants making strong first showings. The impact of the vote for the new Shas party, comprised of pious Orientals which had split off from the Ashkenazi-dominated Agudat, was considerable. With a minimal organization Shas won four Knesset seats and 3.1 percent of the vote. The vote for Agudat was halved. It won only two seats, and its vote was reduced from 3.7 in 1981 to 1.7 percent. In the Knesset Shas would be represented by four young rabbis of Oriental origin, and early indications were that they were less averse to accepting Cabinet posts than Agudat MKs.

The new Morasha party, led by rightwing defectors from the NRP and supported by the Agudat workers' party (PAY), polled 1.6 percent of the vote, gaining two seats. The NRP's vote was reduced to 3.5 percent, and it lost two Knesset seats.

Overall the relative position of the religious camp was slightly improved. It now held 12 seats compared to ten in 1981, and the combined vote for the four parties was 9.9 percent compared to the 8.6 percentage of the two older parties in 1981. It was unlikely, however, the four parties would function as a Knesset bloc. In the process of coalition formation, neither of the two major parties would have enough cabinet posts to accommodate patronage goals of all four. Also the Morasha party under Rabbi Druckman's leadership was more militantly nationalist than the other three.

Gains and losses for the other parties. The position of the two leading left-liberal parties--Rubinstein's Shinui party, heir to Yadin's DMC, and Mrs. Aloni's CRM, markedly improved. In 1981 both had suffered from the polarization of the electorate between Likud and Labor. Shinui polled 2.6 percent of the vote compared to 1.5 in 1981 and increased its Knesset representation from two to three seats. The CRM, reduced to one seat in 1981, won three seats with 2.4 percent of the vote. The winning of six seats by these two small parties was mainly at Labor's expense, which both the CRM and Shinui had savaged during the campaign. They remained, however, Labor's likliest allies in a "narrow" (limited) coalition.

Weizman's centrist Yahad party did less well than expected. Yahad initially had several advantages in the campaign. Weizman was a national political figure and widely popular. His dovish approach was expected to attract some votes from Labor and moderate parties. His campaigning in Arab areas was effective. He enlisted capable lieutenants--retired IDF officers, for his party organization. But Yahad won only 2.2 percent of the vote and three seats in the Knesset. Yet due to the electoral stalemate Weizman could expect to play an important role in negotiations for a new coalition.

Abuhatzeira's Tami party, competing in its second election, suffered a serious setback. It lost two of its three parliamentary seats, and its 1981 percentage of 2.3 percent was reduced to 1.5 percent, i.e. two-fifths of its vote. Its defectors shifted to Shas, Yahad and even to the Alignment. Speculation arose as to whether Tami, heavily reliant on Oriental voters, could survive the competition from the new Shas party with a similar ethnic base. Due to the close election and Abuhatzeira's political skills, the Tami party was expected to play at least a marginal role in coalition-formation.

Of the several one-man parties only ex-Finance Minister Hurvitz' Ometz party won a Knesset seat. Of the 15 successful parties Hurvitz' vote (23,845) was the lowest. His Ometz party appeared to have absorbed some of the vote Dayan's Telem party had won in 1981. Of the 11 parties that failed to qualify, Eliav's dovish party won the highest number of votes, but less than the necessary one percent.

The ethnic vote (Jewish sector). Recent trends in ethnic voting patterns--the marked preference of Oriental voters for the Likud and other right-wing parties and the Ashkenazi preference for

Labor and moderate parties--were replicated in the
1984 election. The Oriental vote for Likud increased only slightly, from 51.6 in 1981 to 52.3
in 1984. But the Likud vote in development towns
of predominantly Oriental population remained
strong. A 1984 voting survey indicated that in
eight representative towns heavily populated by
Orientals, the Likud had a margin over Labor of
more than 2.5 to 1,(32) whereas in eight equiva-
lent towns of mixed population the Likud vote over
Labor was less than 1.2 to 1. The Oriental vote
for Labor declined from 21.2 percent in 1981 to
19.7 in 1984.

Among Ashkenazi voters there was a slight shift
away from the Alignment to other moderate parties.
The percentage of the Ashkenazi vote for the CRM
and Shinui, nominal allies of Labor, increased by
four percent over 1981. An estimated two percent
of the Ashkenazi electorate voted for Weizman's
new Yahad party.(33)

The important new aspect of ethnic voting in
1984 was the impressive first showing of the Shas
party. Of the approximately 15 percent of Oriental Jews that voted for religious parties (including Tami) the Shas party polled nearly half (6.4
percent). The Oriental vote for Shas' parent
party, the Agudat, dropped from four to one percent.(34)

In the past seven years the number of Oriental
Jews holding seats in the Knesset has gradually
increased. In 1977 there were only 22 Oriental
Jews in the Knesset. In 1981 this number was
increased to 27 and in 1984 to 31 members still
only a fourth of the total. Each of the two major
parties presently has ten Oriental MKs.

The Arab vote. For the first time more than
half the Israeli Arabs--52 percent--voted for two
anti-Zionist parties--the Communist Rakah and the
new PLP. In 1977 the Rakah had won an unprecedented 49 percent of the Arab vote, but in 1981

32. Schocken, op. cit., p. 86.

33. *Jerusalem Post,* August 3, 1984.

34. Ibid.

with the electorate more polarized between Likud
and Labor, Rakah's percentage declined to 36 percent. In the 1984 election Rakah's Arab vote
decreased to 34 percent. The major beneficiary of
this shift was the PLP, which in its first electoral try, won 18 percent of the Arab vote and two
Knesset seats. The Rakah no longer monopolized
the anti-Establishment "protest" vote of the
Arabs. Rakah's retention of its four Knesset
seats was due to the increased size of the electorate in 1984, which enabled Rakah to win the
same percentage of the vote--3.4 percent--as in
1981.

In the campaign the PLP charged that Rakah was
not a truly Arab party, because it regularly sponsored an ethnically balanced ticket, one Jew for
every Arab with a Jew, Meir Wilner, heading the
list. Ironically one of the two PLP candidates
elected to the Knesset was an Arab (Miari), and
the other a Jew (General Peled), reflective of the
parity principle which the PLP had adopted. The
PLP's initial electoral success was due mainly to
two factors: a sharp drop in Labor's percentage
of the Arab vote to 21 percent in 1984; and a
marked increase in the Arab turnout from nearly 69
percent in 1981 when an Arab boycott was partially
operative, to 77 percent, nearly as high as the
Jewish turnout. Some observers believed that the
PLP, having made a creditable first showing, was
likely to increase its strength in the next electoral round, eventually becoming the major political vehicle of Israeli Arabs.

Rubinstein's Shinui party got five percent of
the Arab vote; a Druse was No. 3 on its electoral
list. Weizman's Yahad won nearly six percent,
which helped Yahad gain its third Knesset seat.
Weizman had included a prominent local Arab politician on his party list. Even the NRP increased
its Arab vote from three to four percent. As
before the divided Arab vote represented an admixture of ideology (anti-Zionism) and Arab self-
interest (survival needs as a threatened minority.) In the new Knesset there are seven Arab
members compared to the five elected in 1981.

The Kahane phenomenon. Rabbi Kahane's actions
immediately following his election to the Knesset
were provocative.(35) In his Kach party's victory
march through the Arab Old City in Jerusalem, his
supporters, some of whom wore pistols in their
belt holsters, shouted "death to the Arabs" and
"Arabs out." Kahane vowed that his first action
in the Knesset would be to sponsor a bill expel-
ling the 700,000 Israeli Arabs and the 1.3 million
Arabs in the West Bank and Gaza. "Imagine the
pleasure in every heart in the country," he said,
"when I get up and tell Rakah's MK Tawfik Toubi
(an Arab): 'Toubi, today is the day you start
your departure from this country'." In the swear-
ing in of new Knesset members in August, Kahane
equivocated when the acting Speaker insisted that
he affirm allegiance to Israel. Outside the Parliament building more than 2,000 demonstrators
gathered to protest Kahane's entry and denounce
racism.

The most serious post-election incident occurred when supporters of Kahane decided in August to
march on Israel's largest Arab village--Umm al-
Fahn, a center of Arab radicalism with a population of 24,000 persons. Timely police intervention prevented a violent confrontation between
Kahane's supporters and a mixed crowd of 5,000
Arabs and Jews, who had assembled in advance to
deny them entry. It included members of the Knesset, a large contingent of kibbutzim members and
leaders of the leftist peace movement. The police
feared an open clash between the two groups would
set off a wave of violence in other parts of
Israel with large Arab populations.

Public reaction to Kahane's election was extremely negative, although some rightwing leaders
qualified their critical statements.(36) Prime
Minister Shamir called the Kahane phenomenon
"negative, dangerous and harmful," and said that
ways should be found "to limit the damage he could

35. *Jerusalem Post, International Edition,* July 29, September 2,
1984.
36. *Jerusalem Post, International Edition,* September 2, 1984.

cause." In a radio speech Ariel Sharon disassociated himself from Kahane's "actions and words," but added that he regarded radicalism on the left as far more dangerous. A Labor MK (Tzur) said that if there were no law prohibiting Kahane's attacks on Arabs, the Knesset should enact one. A member of the La'am faction (Olmert) argued that no member of the Knesset was entitled to absolute legal immunity if he or she advocated discrimination and expulsion of Israeli citizens. Rabbi Druckman of the rightist Morasha party claimed he would support legislation against incitement, provided it covered incitement by Arabs to get Jews out of Hebron. The Shinui party's council instructed its three MKs to sponsor legislation that would cancel the parliamentary immunity of MKs accused of incitement. Outside Israel, leaders of the American Jewish Congress likened Kahane to Louis Farrakhan (the U.S. Black Muslim minister), and said there was little difference between Kahane's ideology and that of neo-Nazis.

Election surveys showed that Kahane's Kach party relied heavily on Oriental voters, including those dissatisfied with Likud, to pass the one percent threshold.(37) In small development towns Kahane gained 3.3 percent of the total vote and nearly the same amount in religious moshavim with mostly Oriental populations. In slum areas of Jerusalem he drew 2.7 percent, and in large development towns like Beersheba and Ashdod almost two percent. In the older cities with Ashkenazim majorities Kach got only 0.9 percent, less than 0.5 percent in the richer areas of Tel Aviv and Haifa and only a negligible vote in veteran kibbutzim.

37. *Jerusalem Post, International Edition,* July 29, 1984.

(4) The Formation of a National Unity Government

The electoral stalemate raised the urgent question as to what kind of coalition the party leaders could form: a broad coalition, comprised of the two major parties and several lesser parties; a narrow coalition--holding a minimum of 61 seats in the Knesset, led by one of the two major parties and their respective allies; or as a last resort a minority government, formed by the Labor party and its allies with the passive support of the two far left parties, Rakah and the PLP.

At the outset each of the two major parties was preoccupied with organizing a "blocking" coalition--i.e. a coalition supported by 60 MKs that would deprive the opposition party of parliamentary confirmation. Likud with its 41 seats required the support of Tehiya (5 seats), all 12 representatives of the religious parties as well as Hurvitz´ Ometz and Rabbi Kahane´s Kach party. The religious parties were generally disposed to delay their commitment until they extracted maximum concessions from either of the two major parties. In addition to its own 44 seats the Labor alignment needed the six seats of its two allies-- Shinui(3) and CRM(3), Yahad´s three seats, Tami´s single seat and in addition the passive support of the six MKs of the pro-Arab parties. Neither Weizman or Abuhatzeira was inclined to make an early commitment. The difficulties which both Likud and Labor encountered in organizing blocking coalitions accelerated the movement toward a broad coalition including both Likud and Labor.

The proponents of a national unity government argued that the severity of Israel´s economic crisis required a government that transcended narrow partisan interests. Several factors favored the formation of such a government: very substantial public support, as reflected in opinion polls; widespread support by influential newspapers; and President Herzog´s endorsement. Its supporters could point to the precedent of the "wall-to-wall" government set up at the time of the 1967 war, which lasted until 1970. Some secularists were attracted to a unity coalition because it would be less subject to blackmail tactics by the religious parties.

Critics of a broad coalition argued that it would merely paper over important policy differences between Likud and Labor on security and foreign policy questions, and that it would prove to be a short-lived stratagem without having contributed to resolution of Israel's grave problems. Also the two major parties would be unable to agree, it was said, on the distribution of cabinet posts.

A striking feature of the coalition formation process was President Herzog's activist role. In the ten previous elections the Head of State had merely nominated the party leader with the most Knesset seats as Prime Minister-designate. In 1984 the electoral stalemate enhanced the President's discretionary authority, because although Labor was the largest parliamentary party, it was uncertain that Peres could form a narrow coalition. Even before he began his preliminary consultations, President Herzog held special talks with Shamir and Peres, urging them to join in a unity coalition. He also excluded Rabbi Kahane from the consultation process--all the other 14 Knesset parties were included, on grounds of Kahane's extremist views against Israel's Arab minority.

On August 5 the President named Shimon Peres as his first choice to form a government based on national unity. Herzog said a national consensus existed among all parties that Israel's economic situation was the "most dangerous and difficult this state has ever known." He also drew attention to an "absence of tolerance and dialogue" which had received "frightening and disgraceful public expression," endangering Israel's democracy.(38) Herzog gave two reasons for choosing Peres. The Labor party had received nearly 65,000 more votes than Likud, and in his consultations

38. *New York Times*, August 6, 1984.

with Knesset factions, he found more MKs favored Peres over Shamir.

Under the basic law Peres was granted an initial period of 21 days to form a new government, which could be renewed by the President for a second three week period, if required. The coalition negotiations proved difficult, and Peres needed nearly the full time of 42 days.

Although Peres pledged himself to seek a broadly based coalition with the opposition Likud, he simultaneously carried on negotiations for a narrow coalition with smaller parties, should the unity talks collapse. Shamir followed the same two-tier pattern--direct talks with Peres on a unity coalition and separate talks with lesser parties on a Likud-led narrow coalition. The two-tier negotiations tended to slow the unity talks between Peres and Shamir, because both leaders were reluctant to make concessions to each other that would adversely affect their relationships with their usual allies. At several points the Peres-Shamir talks broke down, which served to reactivate their separate talks on forming a narrow coalition.

At the outset of the unity talks expert teams were set up by both sides to prepare position papers on economic and foreign policy questions. By mid-August the two major parties had reached a minimal agreement on guidelines for a future economic policy of drastic retrenchment. Security and foreign policy issues proved less tractable. The Labor delegation favored a freeze on Jewish settlements on the West Bank, although it was willing to "insure their existence." The Likud team wanted to push ahead on an expanded settlement program that the Shamir government had already authorized, and argued that some of the established settlements were so "small and wobbly," that merely "insuring their existence" would lead to their demise.(39) Labor remained deeply opposed to annexation of the occupied territories. On the question of initiating peace negotiations

39. *Jerusalem Post, International Edition*, August 19, 1984.

with Jordan's King Hussein, Labor proposed that
Jordan be invited to peace talks without preconditions, while Likud insisted that Jordanian participation rest on the 1978 Camp David agreement.

The structure and composition of a unity coalition proved a highly contentious issue. What
should be its time limits--one year, 18 months or
the full parliamentary term of four years? Should
it pursue a restricted agenda? How should the key
posts of Prime Minister, Foreign, Defence and
Finance ministers be distributed, and should there
be some system of rotation for some of these
offices between the two parties? Should Peres or
Shamir be the first Prime Minister? Gradually
after prolonged bickering a compromise agreement
emerged. It was proposed that the new unity coalition serve for a period of 50 months until the
next Knesset election in 1988. Peres would serve
as Prime Minister and Shamir as Foreign Minister
for 24 months, at which time the two leaders would
exchange positions. Labor's Rabin would serve as
Defense Minister for the entire period. Likud
would receive most of the important economic ministries, including the Treasury.

During the unity negotiations both parties
continued to woo the smaller parties--both to
strengthen their bargaining positions in the unity
talks and as prospective partners in an alternative narrow coalition. Labor scored an apparent
breakthrough on August 22, when Ezer Weizman decided to merge his Yahad party with the Labor
alignment. Likud had also made strenuous efforts
to enlist Weizman's party on its side. In joining
Labor Weizman reportedly insured himself the No. 5
slot on the Alignment's next electoral list and
several other safe seats for Yahad. Labor not
only had strengthened its position in the next
election, but also increased pressure on Likud to
join a broad coalition. Hurvitz also decided to
affiliate his Ometz party with Labor. But these
gains for Labor were partially offset, when the
NRP and Tami--holding five Knesset seats, announced they would hold out for a unity coalition
that included Likud. Labor had been maneuvering

to persuade the NRP and Tami to join its narrow coalition, if unity talks failed.

Just as final agreement for a unity coalition appeared imminent in mid-September, Shamir was faced with a revolt in his own Herut party. He was sharply criticized for having given away too much to Labor. Shamir's critics favored a one-year rotation of the prime ministership and opposed Rabin's four-year tenure as Defense Minister. At this point Peres hinted that he might abandon his unity efforts and attempt to form a narrow coalition without Likud.

The NRP, which consistently favored a unity government, played a mediatory role in resuscitating a unity agreement with minor modifications. It was provided that a member of the Likud bloc would serve as deputy minister in Rabin's Defense Ministry, and a Labor representative would be deputy Finance Minister.

Peres also faced heavy criticism, when Labor's central committee voted on the unity agreement. Members of Labor's "Young Guard" faction concentrated their fire on four points: the legitimation given Ariel Sharon by naming him to an important cabinet post; Labor's "sell-out" to Likud by granting it the most important economic posts; the unconstitutionality of the plan to rotate the premiership; and Labor's disregard of its socialist ideals by entering a government with rightwing Likud. In reply Peres said the agreement ended seven years of Likud rule and argued it would give Israel a chance to overcome its serious problems. After a heated four-hour debate Labor's central committee approved the unity agreement by a vote of 394 to 166.

The unity negotiations gravely disturbed relations between Labor and its Mapam ally. At their outset Mapam, although it opposed Labor's sharing of governmental power with Likud on ideological grounds, adopted a wait-and-see attitude and deferred a final decision on joining a unity coalition. This postponement considerably strengthened Peres' hand. If Mapam had left the Alignment during Peres' talks with Shamir, Labor's parlia-

mentary position would have been reduced from 44
to 38 seats, three less than Likud. Shamir could
then have justifiably claimed that Labor was no
longer the largest party, and that he should take
charge of the coalition negotiations. Confronted
with Peres' unity agreement, Mapam's central committee voted overwhelmingly--with only six dissenting votes, to reject it. Mapam's leader,
Victor Shemtov, criticized its "very general"
guidelines on economic matters, which would allow
the introduction of many "anti-social and anti-
worker steps."(40) Mapam's negative decision
terminated its 15-year partnership with Labor.
Shemtov held open the door for a future recon-
ciliation, should the unity government collapse.
Some Mapam leaders called for an ideologically
rejuvenated party which could work for a new leftist bloc.

The unity agreement also disturbed relations
between Labor and its left-liberal allies--Shinui
and CRM. CRM's Mrs. Aloni disliked the provision
for a rotating prime ministership, which in her
opinion violated the traditional parliamentary
distinction between government and opposition.
She also argued that despite a Labor party premier, the new government's dominant ideology would
be Herut's. Her Knesset faction decided to vote
against it. A prominent Labor leftwing MK, Yossi
Sarid, quit Labor and joined the CRM, which increased its parliamentary representation to four
seats. Shinui was internally divided. One of its
MKs (Virshubski) abstained in the Knesset vote on
the agreement, but Shinui leader Rubenstein accepted a cabinet post in the new government.

The Likud was also afflicted with internal
frictions over the unity agreement. Shamir's two
leading rivals, Levy and Sharon, harassed Shamir
during the negotiations and claimed he made excessive concessions to Peres. Some observers held
that Sharon opposed a unity coalition, because if
Likud went into opposition, Shamir's position as
party leader could be more readily undermined.

40. *Jerusalem Post, International Edition*, September 16, 1984.

Sharon precipitated a last-minute furor in the
Herut central committee over Shamir´s exclusion of
ex-Finance Minister Aridor from the unity cabinet.
Sharon, joined by Levy, insisted that the proposed
list of Herut ministers be chosen by secret ballot. Sharon´s maneuver failed, and Shamir´s
choices were confirmed.

The unity agreement also cost the Likud bloc
support of its right-wing Tehiya ally. Tehiya MKs
were unwilling to endorse its provisions on future
Jewish settlements (see below).

After seven weeks of wrangling the new unity
cabinet was approved by a Knesset vote of 89-18
with one abstention (in the eight-hour debate 12
MKs left the chamber before the final tally). It
was supported by Labor, Likud and a cluster of
smaller parties representing 97 members.

The new Cabinet. The unity Cabinet was based
on rough approximation of the equality principle.
Ten cabinet seats were assigned to Labor and two
seats to its allies (Shinui and Ometz). Ten seats
were allocated to Likud, divided between Herut and
the Liberals, plus two seats for its allies (Shas
and Morasha). The NRP was given one seat held by
Dr. Burg, who insisted his party was not affiliated with either bloc. The key posts held by
Labor included the office of Prime Minister
(Peres), Defense(Rabin), Education and Culture
(Navon), Economics and Planning(Ya´acobi) and the
newly created Police Ministry(Bar-Lev). Labor´s
new ally, Ezer Weizman, was given a special assignment in the Prime Minister´s office, presumably to seek renewed contacts with Egypt. Shinui´s
Rubinstein was named Minister of Communications,
and Hurvitz, Minister without Portfolio.

In the Likud, a formula was devised for dividing its ten seats between Herut and the Liberals--
roughly one ministry per four MKs: six for Herut,
four for the Liberals. For the Herut Shamir was
both deputy Prime Minister and Foreign Minister;
Levy, vice-premier and Minister of Construction
and Housing; and Sharon, Minister of Industry and
Trade. The critical post of Finance Minister was

assigned to the controversial Liberal leader, Yitzhak Modai. Interestingly neither Peres or Shamir evinced interest in assigning direct responsibility for developing an austerity program to either a Labor or Herut cabinet member. The former Defense Minister, Moshe Arens, was reduced to a ministry without portfolio. Leaders of the two religious parties, Shas and Morasha, were named ministers without portfolio. Due to a patronage dispute between Shas and NRP, the portfolios for the Religious Affairs and Interior ministries were "deposited" with Prime Minister Peres for a limited period until a compromise was worked out between the two parties. Six of the 25 Cabinet members were Oriental Jews.

The Coalition Agreement and policy guidelines. The Coalition Agreement approved by the Knesset formalized the rotation of the offices of Prime Minister and Foreign Minister and specified the ministries assigned to each of the major parties. If other parties later joined the coalition, the same party balance was to be preserved. An inner cabinet of 10 members was created, five for each party, comprised of leading cabinet ministers.

The "Guidelines" dealt mainly with the contentious settlements issue and peace negotiations with Arab states.(41) Most concrete decisions on future Jewish settlements in the occupied territories were left to future cabinet deliberations. Labor was obliged, however, to agree to a half-dozen of the 27 additional settlements approved by the previous Likud government. The unity government would decide on the timing of new settlements, which could only be initiated by a majority of ministers. This provision appeared to give Labor a veto over new settlements. The existence and security of existing settlements was guaranteed, but a decision on their rate of development was subject to cabinet discussions. Neither the West Bank or Gaza could be annexed during the period of the unity government. The Likud had not

41. Ibid.

been able to sustain its militant stance on the settlements question.

Peace talks with the Arabs, which did not appear imminent, were hedged with various restrictions. Opposition to creation of an independent Palestinian state between Israel and the Jordan River was reiterated, and there would be no negotiations with the PLO. Jordan would be invited to enter into peace negotiations with no preconditions specified. If disagreement over the territorial question developed in the peace talks, fresh elections would be held. Diplomatic relations with Egypt should be restored, and negotiations for an autonomous regime in the West Bank under the Camp David agreement resumed. No dramatic peace initiative seemed likely in the near term. On the complicated Lebanese question the Guidelines merely called for an IDF withdrawal (no time limit specified), "while assuring the safety of the Galilee."

Reflecting the weakened position of the religious parties and in contrast to the coalition agreements of 1977 and 1981, the new guidelines merely promised to maintain the status quo on religious matters. The tabling of religious bills by individual MKs would require the approval of both the Prime Minister and deputy Prime Minister. Under the Government's proposed austerity budget, the generous flow of public funds to religious institutions was expected to be curtailed.

Two other items in the Guidelines were of interest. The Government promised to enact a law on racism, but in light of recent iniatives by Jewish terrorists its implementation remained uncertain. A new ministerial committee was proposed for study of the electoral system and to make proposals for amending the elections law. While there was considerable talk of raising the qualifying threshold from one to three or four percent, such an amendment would require very concerted action by both major parties.

In his presentation speech to the Knesset Prime Minister Peres made an eloquent plea for improved relations with Jordan, calling for a "courageous, ongoing dialogue." "Let the Jordan River serve as a source of irrigation for farmers on either side," Peres said, "rather than a body of water across which we hear only threats."

Summary. Recourse to a unity government stemmed from the electoral weakness of the two major parties and the special vulnerabilities of its two chief negotiators--Peres and Shamir. Neither Labor or Likud was in a strong position to form a stable narrow coalition on its own, and were ineluctably drawn to the alternative of a unity government. Both Peres and Shamir recognized that without a broad coalition, their personal political fortunes were in jeopardy. Peres had led his party to two defeats in 1977 and 1981 and to an uncertain victory in 1984. If he failed to discharge his mandate to organize a unity government, his prestige would be severely, if not fatally damaged. If Likud were pushed into the opposition, Shamir would be an easy target for his ambitious rivals--Sharon and Levy.

The profile of the 11th Knesset was radically changed by the advent of a unity government. More than three quarters of its seats were held by a powerful centrist bloc. The small parties on the far left and extreme right were reduced mainly to sniping tactics against the Government, no matter how vociferous their attacks. Real decision-making power was expected to be exerted by the small number of Labor and Likud leaders in the inner cabinet. The Government's future coherence rested on several imponderables: Shamir's capacity to maintain his precarious hold on the Herut leadership; whether Peres and Shamir could establish a satisfactory working relationship on a day-to-day basis; whether the momentum towards an expanded settlement program could be checked by the Government; whether so unwieldy a coalition could take the requisite bold steps to counteract the severe economic deterioration; and whether Syria would act to facilitate an early Israeli withdrawal from Lebanon.

A significant feature of the unity negotiations

was the relatively minor role played by the lesser
parties. They received, despite strenuous efforts, modest patronage pay-offs. The divided
religious camp was unable to make a unified bid
for the important post of Minister of Religious
Affairs. Ezer Weizman had initially been expected
to play a pivotal role in coalition formation and
secure for himself a top cabinet position, but he
ended up with a special assignment of uncertain
importance. Tami's Abuhatzeira, who outdid all
his rivals in efforts to extract maximum patronage
gains for his one-man party, in the end gained
nothing.

In addition to single cabinet seats won by
Shas, Morasha and the NPR, the Agudat got a deputy
ministership (Porush) and chairmanship of the
powerful Knesset Finance Committee (Shapira).
Should the unity coalition falter, however, the
religious parties could be expected to reactivate
their parochial claims with renewed vigor.

The introduction of the parity principle in
allocation of cabinet positions and a rotation
system for two high governmental offices were an
unusual innovation in Israeli politics. Some
Likud leaders feared the unity government would
collapse before Shamir had his turn as Prime Minister, and that Peres would push Shamir into the
background on important foreign policy matters.
Considering the Likud's previously dismal record
on economic policy, there was irony in Likud's
gaining the most important economic post.

With its limited agenda and policy guidelines
based on the lowest common denominator, the new
Government was widely considered Israel's least
ideological. There is a seeming paradox in the
markedly low ideological content of the Coalition
Agreement and continued evidence that religious
fervor combined with expansionist nationalism is
at high tide in Israel. Whether a compromise
coalition could contain these powerful forces
remained problematic.

V
Electoral Trends
A Summary

Most academic studies of Israeli elections deal
with single elections, are collaborative works to
which several specialists contribute, are directed
mainly though not exclusively to other specialists
and increasingly employ a strict behavioral approach.   This nontechnical study of three Israeli
elections is intended as an introductory study for
American undergraduates and the general reader.
It assumes that serious study of three successive
elections in a particularly volatile period in
Israeli politics will yield tentative generaliza-
tions regarding important electoral trends.   These
are summarized in this concluding chapter.

The trend toward a competitive party system.
The historic function of the 1977 election was to
terminate the long political ascendancy of the
Labor party.   Labor won the support of only about
a quarter of the electorate.   Yadin's new party,
the DMC, provided a catchall refuge for disaffected Labor voters.   Winning a third of the electorate and 43 Knesset seats, the Likud became for
the first time a viable governing party.   In 1981
the Labor party made a substantial recovery, increasing its popular vote by 12 points (36.6 percent of the vote).   In a polarized electorate

Labor and Likud received approximately the same
percentage of the popular vote and had parliamentary delegations of nearly equal size (Likud--48
seats, Labor 47). Together the two major parties
won nearly 80 percent of the Knesset seats and 75
percent of the popular vote. The electorate's
rightward drift gave Likud the advantage in forming a narrow coalition. Despite the overall diminished vote of the lesser parties, the virtual
deadlock between the major parties enabled several
of the lesser parties to retrieve their prestige
by joining Begin's second government.

In 1984 in contrast to the polarization of the
vote in 1981, there occurred a significant splintering of the electorate, especially on the right
and left extremes, which weakened the position of
both the major parties. In this instance Labor
and Likud controlled 70 percent of Knesset seats,
a drop of nearly 10 percent over 1981. Thirteen
of the smaller parties met the one percent requirement compared to 11 parties in 1981. On the
extreme right two parties held six seats (Tehiya's
five, Kahane's one), compared to Tehiya's three
seats in 1981, which partly explains Likud's loss
of seven seats. On the far left Rakah's electoral
front retained four seats, and the new Arab Progressive List won two seats. After the formation
of the new unity government the left opposition
was further strengthened by addition of the Mapam
party's six seats. Labor's loss of three seats
resulted in gains for its left-liberal and more
dovish allies, the CRM and Shinui, each winning
three seats, and contributed to the winning of
three seats by Weizman's new Yahad party. Although the total vote for the religious camp did
not change substantially, it was divided among
four parties rather than two as in 1981. The
decline in the vote for the two established religious parties, NRP and Agudat, mainly explains the
relatively good showing of the two new parties,
Shas and Morasha. The notable splintering of the
electorate in 1984 and weakened position of Likud
and Labor provided a powerful momentum for the
formation of a unity government. Most observers

predicted that if the new unity government proved short-lived and led to fresh elections, the inconclusive results that characterized both the 1981 and 1984 elections would be replicated. These expectations indicated that the present competitive phase of the party system is likely to persist for an indefinite period.

The continued importance of the floating vote. In each of the three elections the floating vote has been a significant factor in the outcome. In 1977 Labor suffered sweeping defections almost across the board. Even some Likud voters shifted to the DMC. In 1981 with the DMC no longer a contender there was a substantial return of Labor's regular voters, but with Likud's improved showing, these were insufficient to allow Labor to regain its ascendancy. Labor's gains were mainly costly to the CRM and Shinui and led to the demise of the dovish Shelli party and Labor's one-time ally, the ILP. In 1984 the splintering of the vote reflected the enhanced importance of the floating vote. Both Labor and Likud suffered serious defections. There was a significant shift in the Arab vote to the new PLP and to a lesser degree to the Yahad party. Substantial numbers of voters in the religious camp, especially Oriental Jews, transferred their support to the new Shas and Morasha parties.

Certain factors reinforce the trend toward a volatile electorate and a significant floating vote as follows: the continued long-term decline in ideology; the transiency of some small parties which survive for only one or two elections; the progressive urbanization and mobility of immigrant voters; the variable saliency of the peace issue. Obviously the high incidence of the floating vote is a destabilizing factor and deterrent to the emergence of a new dominant party.

The fragility of the major electoral blocs and their leadership succession crises. Both major parties are subject to adverse centrifugal forces which have become more acute in the present tran-

sitional phase. In both parties internal policy
differences, patterns of uninspired leadership and
recurrent power rivalries have a markedly divisive
effect.

(1) *Labor's Divisions*. For more than a decade
hawk-dove differences on the territorial question
have divided the Labor alignment. Labor doves
favor a territorial compromise with Arab states,
the acceptance of some kind of Palestinian state
and restrictions on Jewish settlements in the
occupied territories. Labor hawks hew to a hard
line on the territorial question, in some cases
not dissimilar from that of the Likud, have grave
doubts about the feasibility of a Palestinian
state on Israel's borders and in some cases support the Gush Emunim program for expanded Jewish
settlements. On economic policy the Labor left
favors an expanded public sector, continued support for agricultural collectives and a dynamic
reassertion of socialist ideology, while the
center-right is identified with the maintenance of
a mixed economy with special attention to expanding exports. Mapam's secession in 1984 gave Labor
greater coherence in the short term, but weakened
it electorally. Important factional differences
on the territorial question remain, and party
support for a controlled economy and wage-price
freezes is soft.

Labor's leadership succession crisis remains
unresolved. In 1977 Rabin's temporary retirement
from government gave Peres an important advantage
in their ongoing rivalry. Control of the party
machine enabled Peres to play the leading role in
reorganizing the party after its stunning defeat
in 1977. In 1981 Rabin, although defeated for the
party leadership, made strenuous efforts to protect his factional interests in forming Labor's
electoral lists and was able to extract a last-
minute promise of the Defense Ministry for himself, should Labor win the election.

Prior to the 1984 election a new contender for
party leadership emerged, when former President
Navon returned to active politics. With Oriental
Jews constituting a majority of the electorate,

Navon's ethnic status was considered an advantage. With considerable skill Peres was able to fend off another bitter contest over party leadership and present a united party to the electorate. Peres was unable, however, to lead his party to a decisive victory. His present position as Prime Minister of an unwieldy unity coalition is precarious. Both Rabin and Navon hold powerful positions in the cabinet--Rabin as Defense Minister and Navon as Education Minister, from which they can monitor Peres' performance.

(2) *Frictions in the Likud.* Menachem Begin's precipitous retirement in 1983 exacerbated the ongoing power rivalries in the Herut leadership over his succession. Begin's successor as Prime Minister, Shamir, had two major rivals--Levy and Sharon. Shamir's performance as head of government was unexceptional. He attempted with limited success to stave off the most damaging effects of Israel's severe economic crisis and keep the lid on the explosive Lebanese situation. His role as low-keyed leader of Likud's unimpressive campaign had mixed results--a substantial loss of votes compared to 1981, but less disastrous than the polls predicted. Herut's power struggle continued unabated during the delicate unity negotiations with both Levy and Sharon sharply criticizing Shamir's concessions to Labor. The commitment of the latter two to the unity government, despite their acceptance of cabinet positions, seemed equivocal at best. Shamir's fate was closely linked to the longevity of the new unity government. His leadership of Herut was certain to be challenged in the party's next convention, probably in the spring of 1985. If either Sharon or Levy--or possibly Moshe Arens, should replace Shamir in the near future, the position of Herut's new leader would be far from secure.

Sharon had played a catalytic role in the formation of Likud in 1973. In the first Begin government he was closely identified with an assertive pro-settlement policy. In the second Begin government he was the principal strategist in Israel's bold attempt to convert Lebanon into a

satellite regime and eliminate Syria as a serious
rival there. Despite his enforced resignation as
Defense Minister, the resourceful Sharon managed
to remain a leading contender for Herut leadership
and win an important post in the unity government.
For nearly a decade Sharon has been the scourge of
liberal Israelis as a political leader with con-
tempt for constitutional niceties. His promotion
to Prime Minister would be widely regarded as a
turning point in Israeli politics.

Even before the 1981 election Likud's rightwing faction, dissatisfied with Begin's concessions in peace negotiations with Egypt, had split
off to form the independent Tehiya party. Although Tehiya joined the second Begin government
in 1982, differences over security issues remained. As one arm of the settlement movement,
Tehiya attracted increasing support of ultranationalist voters. In the unity negotiations
Tehiya refused to support Shamir's concessions to
Labor on the settlements question and became the
core of the rightist opposition to the government.

As the 1984 campaign demonstrated, Herut's
relationship with its Liberal allies was subject
to heavy strains. Some Herut leaders viewed the
Liberals as a political liability, whose control
of a dozen Knesset seats grossly exaggerated their
contribution to the Likud vote. If the seriously
factionalized Liberals competed in the next election as an independent party, they would be
reduced, it was said, to a minor parliamentary
faction. Other Herut leaders, more cautious in a
time of declining fortunes for the Likud, were
reluctant to cut the Liberals adrift. Some observers predicted, however, that the Likud alliance
would in fact be dissolved before the next election. The performance of Liberal leader Modai as
Finance Minister in the unity government could
prove to be an important factor in determining the
future coherence of the Likud bloc.

The variable importance of the ethnic vote.
The present transitional period has witnessed an
historic assertiveness of the increasingly influ-

ential voting power of Oriental Jews to the disadvantage of the Ashkenazi Establishment, especially in the Labor leadership. For reasons considered above, Begin's Herut party became their principal political vehicle. The previous electoral record of ethnic parties organized exclusively on an ethnic basis was unimpressive. For many Orientals the Likud had the attraction of riding the crest of an unprecedented wave of expansionist nationalism, focused on retention of the occupied territories. Most importantly Begin succeeded in establishing an unusual rapport with a large segment of the Oriental electorate. The one-time pariah political leader coalesced with the "second Israel," whose members were bent on redressing accumulated grievances against the Ashkenazi elite. The climax of this identification came in the turbulent 1981 election with the outbreak of violent street demonstrations against Peres and other leaders of the Ashkenazi-dominated Alignment. With the Likud Government's placatory attitude toward the Orientals and Begin's retirement from politics, there was in 1984 a subsidence in the violent expression of ethnic tensions. Ethnic militance was expressed, however, in a new arena with the formation of the new Shas party, led by Orientals, as a splinter off the Ashkenazi-led Agudat. Speculation was rife that Shas' winning of four Knesset seats in its first electoral effort foreshadowed further decline in the fortunes of the NRP and Agudat and an important realignment of forces in the religious camp. It also cast doubt on the future viability of an earlier Oriental splinter, the Tami party.

It is probable that the present voting preference of many Oriental Jews for the Likud will prove a transient phenomenon. The shift in the Oriental vote to Likud was partly conceived as an effective device to punish the Labor party for its leadership's patronizing attitudes toward Oriental immigrants, which may prove an insufficient motivation for long-term affiliation to Likud. Orientals are still strikingly underrepresented in government and party bodies and remain a relative-

ly depressed sector in the economy. Disillusionment with Likud may follow disillusionment with
Labor, and lead to the search for a more effective
party vehicle to establish the Orientals' political ascendancy which their growing numbers por-
tend.

   Shifting allegiances in the Arab sector. In
recent elections the bulk of the Arab vote has
been divided between Rakah and the Labor party
with its affiliated Arab lists and scattered
voting for other parties. In the 1970s there was
a significant radicalization of the Arab electorate as Israeli Arabs became more closely identified with their Arab brothers in the occupied
territories. The Communist Rakah became an especially vocal champion of Arab interests, as seen
in their prominent role in organizing the Arab
Land Day demonstrations in 1976. In 1977 Rakah's
percentage of the Arab vote increased 12 percentage points to an unprecedented 49 percent. More
and more Rakah was becoming the primary vehicle of
an Arab protest vote against the Government's
indifference to Arab interests. Labor got 27
percent of the Arab vote.
   But in 1981 with the sharp polarization of the
vote between Likud and Labor, a significant number
of Arab voters decided that the Begin government's
Arab policies were considerably worse than its
Labor predecessor, making it imperative to oppose
Likud's return to office. The Arab vote for Labor
increased from 27 percent to 36 percent, and the
Arab vote for Rakah dropped for the first time
since 1961, from 49 percent in 1977 to 36 percent
in 1981. The decline in Rakah's vote was partly
attributed to the election boycott called by
radical Arab groups. The boycott also adversely
affected the usually high Arab turnout which
dropped to a low of 69 percent.
   The new element affecting the Arab vote in 1984
was the entry of the PLP. Arab turnout increased
eight points to 77 percent. The PLP claimed 18
percent of the Arab vote, Rakah's share dropped

slightly to 34 percent and Labor's vote significantly declined to 21 percent.

As the vote for the PLP is expected to increase in future elections, it may indirectly affect the formation of future coalition governments. If the number of PLP MKs increases, it will automatically increase the number of non-coalitional parties, i.e. those that cannot be seriously considered as coalition partners in any government, and introduce fresh complications in coalition formation.

Israel's immediate political future is fraught with uncertainties which will severely test the flexibility and durability of its multiparty democracy. Will the new unity government be sufficiently united to implement an economic policy which requires a considerable reduction in workers' living standards? Will the government succeed in negotiating a satisfactory withdrawal of IDF forces from Lebanon which Syria will sanction? Will the unity government be able to survive its own internal stresses, especially a destabilizing upheaval within the Herut leadership? Can the government withstand renewed pressure from a second Reagan administration to take a more accommodating position on the territorial question? What concrete steps will be taken to implement Peres' promise to improve "the quality of life" for the Arab minority and prevent their further disaffection? Faced with a divided public opinion on Jewish terrorist organizations, will the Government be able to deal decisively with their future strikes? Will the governing parties take practical steps to improve radically their accessibility to Oriental Jews? Given the daunting complexity of these extremely serious problems, will Israel's democratic system meet their challenge or alternatively be found wanting and succeeded by a more authoritarian system?

Selected Bibliography

Books

Arian, Asher. *Ideological Change in Israel.*
Cleveland: Press of Case Western Reserve
University, 1968.
_____, ed. *The Elections in Israel-1973.*
Jerusalem Academic Press, 1975.
_____, ed. *The Elections in Israel-1977.*
Jerusalem Academic Press, 1980.
_____, ed. *The Elections in Israel-1981.*
Tel Aviv: Ramon Publishing Co., 1983.
Aronoff, Myron J. *Power and Ritual in the Israel
Labor Party.* Assen: Van Gorcum, 1977.
Belloni, Frank P. and Beller, Dennis C. *Faction
Politics: Political Parties and Factionalism
in Comparative Perspective.* Santa Barbara,
Ca.: ABC-Clio, Inc., 1978.
Benvenisti, Meron. *The West Bank Data Project:
A Survey of Israel's Policies.* Washington,
D.C.: American Enterprise Institute, 1984.
Bradley, C. Paul. *Electoral Politics in Israel:
The Knesset Election of 1981.* Grantham, N.H.:
Tompson & Rutter Inc., 1981.
Caspi, D., Diskin, A. and Gutman, E., eds. *The
Roots of Begin's Success.* London and Canberra:
Croom Helm, 1984.

Deshen, Shlomo. *Immigrant Voters in Israel.*
Manchester: Manchester University Press, 1970.

Eisenstadt, S.N. *Israeli Society.* New York:
Basic Books, Inc., 1967.

Eisenstadt, S.N., Bar Yosef, Rivah, and Adler,
Chaim, eds. *Integration and Development in
Israel.* Israel Universities Press, 1970.

Fein, Leonard. *Israel: Politics and People.*
Boston: Little, Brown, & Co., 1967.

Freedman, Robert O., ed. *Israel in the Begin Era.*
New York: Praeger, 1982.

Horowitz, Dan and Lissak, Moshe. *The Origins of
the Israeli Polity.* Chicago: University of
Chicago Press, 1980.

Isaac, Rael Jean. *Israel Divided: Ideological
Politics in the Jewish State.* Baltimore:
Johns Hopkins University Press, 1976.

_____. *Party and Politics in Israel: Three
Visions of a Jewish State.* New York: Longman,
1981.

Landau, Jacob. *The Arabs in Israel.* London:
Oxford Press, 1969.

Lehman-Wilzig, Sam N. and Susser, Bernard. *Comparative Jewish Politics: Public Life in Israel
and the Diaspora.* Tel Aviv: Bar-Ilan University Press, 1981.

Liebman, Charles S. and Don-Yehiya, Eliezer.
Religion and Politics in Israel. Bloomington,
Ind.: Indiana University Press, 1984.

Likhouski, Eliahus S. *Israel's Parliament: The
Law of the Knesset.* London: Oxford University
Press, 1971.

Lustick, Ian. *Arabs in the Jewish State.* Austin:
University of Texas Press, 1980.

Mahler, Gregory S. *The Knesset: Parliament in the
Israeli Political System.* London: Associated
University Presses, 1981.

Medding, Peter Y. *Mapai in Israel: Political
Organization and Government in a New Society.*
Cambridge: Cambridge University Press, 1972.

Penniman, Howard R. *Israel at the Polls: The
Knesset Elections of 1977.* Washington, D.C.:
American Enterprise Institute, 1979.

Peretz, Don. *The Government and Politics of Israel*. Boulder, Colo.: Westview Press, 2nd edition, 1983.

Peri, Yoram. *Between Ballots and Bullets: Israeli Military in Politics*. Cambridge: Cambridge University Press, 1983.

Rayman, Paula. *The Kibbutz Community and Nation-Building*. Princeton: Princeton University Press, 1981.

Rothenberg, Gunther E. *The Anatomy of the Israeli Army*. London: B.T.Batsford, Ltd., 1979.

Rubinstein, Amnon. *The Zionist Dream Revisited: From Herzl to Gush Emunim and Back*. New York: Schocken Books, 1984.

Sachar, Howard M. *A History of Israel*. New York: A.A. Knopf, 1976.

Safran, Nadav. *Israel: The Embattled Ally*. Cambridge: Harvard University Press, 1978.

Schiff, Gary S. *Tradition and Politics: The Religious Parties of Israel*. Detroit: Wayne University Press, 1977.

Schiff, Ze'ev and Ya'ari, Ehud. *Israel's Lebanon War*. New York: Simon and Schuster, 1984.

Schnall, David J. *Radical Dissent in Contemporary Israeli Politics: Cracks in the Wall*. New York: Praeger Publ., 1974.

Shama, Avraham and Tris, Mark. *Immigration without Integration: Third World Jews in Israel*. Cambridge, Mass.: Schenkman Co., 1977.

Silver, Eric. *Begin: The Haunted Prophet*. New York: Random House, 1984.

Smooha, Sammy. *Israel: Pluralism and Conflict*. Berkeley: University of California Press, 1978.

Articles

Arian, Asher and Samuel H. Barnes. "The Dominant Party System: A Neglected Model of Democratic Stability." *Journal of Politics* 36 no. 3 (1974).

Avruch, Kevin A. "Gush Emunim Politics, Religion and Ideology in Israel." *Middle East Review* 11 no. 2 (1978-79).

Deshen, Shlomo. "Israeli Judaism: Introduction to the Major Patterns." *International Journal of Middle East Studies* 9, no. 2 (1978).

Dowty, Alan. "Israel: A Time of Retrenchment." *Current History* 83, no. 489 (1984).

Hoffman, Steven A. "Candidate Selection in Israel's Parliament: The Realities of Change." *Middle East Journal* 34, no. 3 (1980).

Nachmias, David. "Coalition Politics in Israel." *Comparative Political Studies* 7, no. 3 (1974).

Oren, Stephen. "Continuity and Change in Israel's Religious Parties." *Middle East Journal* 27, no. 1 (1973).

Peretz, Don. "The Earthquake--Israel's Ninth Knesset Election." *Middle East Journal* 31, no. 3 (1977).

_____. "The War Election and Israel's Eighth Knesset." *Middle East Journal* 28, no. 2 (1974).

_____. "Israel's 1969 Election: The Visible and the Invisible." *Middle East Journal* 24, no. 1 (1970).

Schocken, Gershon. "Israel in Election Year 1984." *Foreign Affairs* 63, no. 1 (1984).

Sprinzak, Ehud. "Extreme Politics in Israel." *The Jerusalem Quarterly* no. 5 (Fall 1977).

Waller, Harold M. "Israel and the Peace Process." *Current History* 82, no. 480 (1983).

Index

formation, 77; votes in, 48, 86, 92, 141, 145, 148, 184

Kook, Rabbis A. Y. and Zvi: and Gush Emunim, 46

Kupat Holim (Sick Fund), 12, 32, 49

La'am faction (Likud), 59, 125, 133-34

Labor party, 49, 51, 68, 89-90, 97-98, 108-9, 139, 145, 148, 189-96; campaign strategy of, 160-61; and coalition formation, (1984) 178-87; and election results, (1977) 61-65, 70-71, 76, (1981) 111-14, 117, (1984) 168, 170, 175; factional divisions of, 41-43, 192-93; formation of, 14; and Histadrut elections, 71, 92; and leadership succession, 38-40, 49, 100-101, 192-93; positions on issues, (1977) 53, (1981) 110-11, (1984) 162-64; and slatemaking, (1977) 59-60, (1981) 107-8, (1984) 152. See also Mapai/Labor and Alignment

Lahad, General Antoine, 164

Lamifne faction (NRP), 55-57, 91

Land Day demonstrations, 68, 157

Land of Israel movement, 45, 165

Leadership, 24; personality factor, 122-23; use of military professionals, 76

Lebanon: crises over (1982), 94-97, 124, 132; and Gemayel government, 140; invasion of (1982), 135-36; and May 17th Agreement (1983), 140-42; withdrawal from, 163-64, 186

Lechi ("Stern gang"), 28

Levinson, Yaacov, 100, 107

Levy, David, 82, 139, 145, 161, 183-84; and Herut leadership succession, 129, 144, 149, 193; and Herut slatemaking, 106, 151

Liberal party, 14, 52-53, 67; and coalition formation, (1981) 125-26, (1984) 184-85; decline of, 133; factionalism in, 88; relations with Herut, 150-51; and Likud slatemaking, (1977) 59, (1981) 106, (1984) 150-51

Likud Utmura faction (NRP), 55-57

Likud bloc, 8, 26, 35, 41, 43, 75, 109, 144-45, 153, 189-97; and coalition formation, (1977) 77-84, (1981) 124-33, (1984) 178-87; election results, (1977) 61-65, 76, (1981) 111-14, 117, (1984) 168-70; factional disputes of, 85-87; formation of, 16; and Histadrut elections, 72, 92; and leadership succession, 193-94; legitimation of, 74; positions on issues, (1977) 52-53, (1981) 110-11, (1984) 162-64; and slatemaking, (1977) 58-59, (1981) 105-106, (1984) 150-51. See also Herut and Liberal party

Livni, Menachem, 165

Lorincz, Shlomo, 156

Mapai/Labor, 8, 31, 73; and civil service, 30-31; and coalition formation, 25-26; as dominant party, 25; and foreign policy, 19-20; and Histadrut, 12; ideology of, 13-14, 18; and IDF, 28-29; leadership succession, 38-40; and use of Arab affiliated lists, 37. See also Labor party

Mapam party, 68, 141; and
foreign policy, 19, 41;
ideology of, 18; and Palm-
ach militia, 28-29; seces-
sion from Labor alignment,
182-83; slatemaking in
Alignment, 23, 152
Massacre at Sabra and Shatilla camps, 137-39
Meir, Golda, 39-40, 69, 72,
73-74
Meridor, Ya'acov, 106
Miari, Mohammed, 156-57
Ministry of Education and
Culture, 80-81
Ministry of Religious Af-
fairs, 16, 31, 32, 71,
81, 127, 188
Mitterand, Francois, 98, 100
Mizrachi party, 30
Modai, Yitchak, 88, 141,
151, 184-85, 194
Morasha party, 154, 172,
185, 190
Moshavim cooperatives, 11,
45, 47
Movement for National Poli-
tical Revival (NRP fac-
tion), 56-57

National Religious party (NRP),
16-18, 37. 74, 75, 190, 195;
and cabinet posts, 16, 31,
81, 128-29, 184-85; and coalition formation, 25-26,
(1977) 80-81, 83, (1981)
123-24, 126-33, (1984)
181-82, 186; election re-
sults, (1977) 61, 65-66, 71,
(1981) 115, 122, (1984) 171-
72, 175; factional divis-
ions in, 41, 46, 54-57, 91,
104-105, 154-56; and Gush
Emunim, 46; and Rabin government, 48-49; and religious schools, 30; and "Who
is a Jew?" question, 19,69
National unity government:
(1967-70), 26, 74; nego-
tiations for (1984), 178-
88; proposals for, 145,
164

Navon Yitzhak, 124, 127, 150,
152, 192-93
Ne'eman, Yuval, 103, 115, 139,
141, 166
Nominations, 23, 51-52, (1977)
57-60, (1981) 105-108,
(1984) 150-52

Ometz party (Courage to Cure
the Economy), 159, 173
Opinion polls, 61, 75, 90,
92-93, 97, 98, 114, 142-43,
166, 168
Oriental (Sephardim) Jews, 18,
26, 31-33, 51, 74, 109, 170;
grievances of, 34-35; and
Kach, 177; and Likud, 75,
93, 106, 121, 143-44, 161,
167, 195-96; and Shas, 174;
and Tami, 105, 115, 121;
vote of, (1977) 64-65,
(1981) 116-17, (1984) 174

Palestine Liberation Organization (PLO), 27, 52, 94,
135-36, 142, 157, 186
Palmach, 28-29
Party system: competitive,
120-21, 189-91; dominant,
73-74, 76-77; movement-
type, 11-12
Party lists, 20-22, 23
Patt, Gideon, 88
Peace Now movement, 45, 90,
138-39
Peled, General Matti, 157
Peres, Shimon, 24, 60, 107;
and campaign violence,
108-109; and coalition
violence (1984), 179-88;
and debate with Begin
(1981), 54, 110-11, 114;
as Defense Minister, 50,
67; as opposition leader,
89, 98, 122-23, 132, 141,
148, 152, 162-65, 170; and
Rafi, 39; and rivalry with
Rabin, 40, 49, 74, 76, 150,
192

Peres government, 184–85, 187, 197

Phalangists, Lebanese, 95; and Sabra and Shatilla massacres, 137–38

Poali Agudat Yisrael party (PAY), 17, 48; election results, (1977) 65–66, (1981) 116; and Morasha, 154

Porush, Rabbi Menahem, 156

Progressive List for Peace (PLP), 156–57, 190–91, 196–97; banning of, 159–60; election results, (1984) 171, 174–75

Progressive National Movement (PNM), 120

Rabin, Yitzhak, 76; as Prime Minister, 40, 48–49, 55–57, 67, 69, 95, 157; rivalry with Peres, 49, 74, 89, 100–101, 107, 150, 192–93

Rabin government, dissolution of, 48–50

Rafi faction, 14, 23, 39, 73, 104

Rakah party, 37, 67; and Arabs, 37–38, 68–69, 70, 119–20, 174–75; election results, (1977) 68–69, (1981) 120, (1984) 171, 174–75

Raphael, Yitzhak, 55–57

Reagan, President Ronald, 96

Religion, 52–53; and concessions to religious parties, (1977) 80–81, (1981) 129, 130–31, 133, (1984) 186; and status quo agreement, 17, 144, 186; "Who is a Jew?" controversy, 19, 69, 81, 126, 129

Revisionist Zionists, 14–15

Rubenstein, Amnon, 51, 84, 88–89, 116, 184. See also Shinui

Sadat, Anwar, 85, 90, 93, 97, 111

Sarid, Yosi, 183

Saudi Arabia, 96

Sawyer, David, 123

Schmidt, Chancellor Helmut, 93–94

Settlements (in occupied territories), 41–42, 46, 49, 52, 133, 144, 147, 149, 154, 162–63, 169, 180, 185–86, 192

Shamir, Yitzhak: and coalition formation, (1983) 144–46, (1984) 178–87; as Foreign Minister, 87, 138, 184; as Herut leader, 148, 151; and Herut leadership succession, 139, 144, 149, 193–94; as Prime Minister, 135, 144–45, 166, 176,

Sharon, General Ariel, 76, 82, 87, 141, 148, 167, 177, 182; as Defense Minister, 129–30, 135–39; and formation of Likud, 16, 67; and leadership succession (Herut), 106, 139, 144, 149–50, 151, 193–94; and massacres at Sabra and Shatilla, 138–39; and military career, 66, 130; and Shlomzion party, 66–67; and war in Lebanon, 136

Shas (Sephardi Tora Guardians) party, 185, 190–91, 195; formation of, 154–55; vote for, (1984) 172, 174

Shelli (Peace for Israel) party, 67–68, 71, 75, 115, 191

Shemtov, Victor, 152, 183

Shinui (Change) party, 50–51, 58, 75, 84, 88–89, 102, 177, 190–91; and coalition formation (1984), 183; election results, (1981) 116, 122, (1984) 172–73, 175

Shlomzion (Peace for Zion) party, 66–67. See also Sharon